LOVING ANIMALS

LOVING ANIMALS

On Bestiality, Zoophilia
and Post-human Love

Joanna Bourke

REAKTION BOOKS

For Costas

Published by
REAKTION BOOKS LTD
Unit 32, Waterside
44–48 Wharf Road
London N1 7UX, UK
www.reaktionbooks.co.uk

First published 2020
Copyright © Joanna Bourke 2020

Printed and bound in Great Britain
by TJ Books Limited, Padstow, Cornwall

A catalogue record for this book is available from the British Library

ISBN 978 1 78914 310 2

CONTENTS

Preface

Anyone who writes books and teaches for a living is constantly being asked: what are you currently working on? I am often reticent about responding, largely because 'my' topics are often uncomfortable ones to talk about: they include killing, combat, dismemberment, militarism, rape, fear, pain and what it means to be human, to name a few. I have become accustomed to awkward silences and quizzical looks.

This book is no different. Its themes follow logically from those that have always fascinated me. Violence is at the heart of all of my writings. How could it be otherwise? After all, humans are extraordinarily cruel.

But I have also learnt that most people possess deep reservoirs of tenderness and love. We all strive to understand others, as well as ourselves. Without human friendships, we would die. If emotional attachments to non-human animals were forbidden, our lives would be incredibly impoverished. The human and non-human animals with whom we engage on a daily basis are our lifeblood.

In the past decade or so, I have been thinking about such relationships. How do sentient creatures express affection for each other? How do we both acknowledge and respect the agency of others? What is so mutually exhilarating about being touched and touching? It is so easy to mistake consent: even in the most heart-warming relationships, power always intrudes. What does it mean to love?

This book does not claim to have answers, but it does hope to provoke discussion about these questions. It does this by tracing through some of the complex and sometimes tricky aspects of our relationships to companion species. The introduction begins by exploring a paradox: for millennia, human–animal sex has been a prominent theme in art and literature, yet it is routinely said to be a 'taboo'. Chapter One looks at legal and religious views about bestiality. Are prohibitions about human–animal sex more about the emotions of disgust and fear than ideological precept? Many readers will find the second chapter painful to read: it explores the sexual abuse of non-human and human animals. I can only encourage readers to persevere with this chapter because it is a central argument of this book that the degradation and sexual abuse of girls, women and non-human animals are linked. Chapter Three turns to the medicalization of interspecies sexual intercourse, culminating in the diagnosis of 'zoophilia' or the (sexual) love of animals. Some self-proclaimed animal-lovers (as I show in Chapter Four) have taken these psychiatric ideas further: they insist that zoophilia is a sexual orientation like homosexuality. Calling themselves 'zoos', these men and women seek public recognition of their sexual identity. The book concludes with a chapter asking: what is the way through this maze? It is not enough to merely *critique* political and ethical positions on human–animal sexuality; people and 'pets' are already in dialogue. How can we create more equitable, fulfilling and erotic worlds for everyone? It is the fundamental tenet of this book that queer theory, post-human philosophy, disability studies and the history of the senses can help move the debates forward.

There is a risk that careless readers might see in my arguments either a defence of the kind of harmful, violent interspecies sex that has typified human–non-human relationships over centuries ('bestiality') or an endorsement of the more recent identity politics of self-proclaimed zoos. I am saying neither. Rather, this book is an attempt to think through ways of cultivating more kind and caring relationships between different species. It pays homage to the possibilities of interspecies understanding and, in the future to come, the promise of love.

Jean-Honoré Fragonard, *Girl with a Dog*, c. 1770, oil on canvas.

Introduction

Define: **Loving.**
The act of expressing love; sexual feelings etc.

J ean-Honoré Fragonard's *Girl with a Dog* was painted around 1770. The painting is typical of his decadent style, with its warm tones, luxuriant brushwork and energetic celebration of pleasure. In the painting, a young girl lies back on her bed, holding a small spaniel whose tail moves between her legs, caressing her vulva and buttocks. Its phallic energy is palpable. The girl's bedside table is open, a visual allegory of her receptivity to sensual advances. The cool blue ribbon of the girl's nightcap is echoed in the bow of the spaniel: the two beautiful creatures are in harmony. The artist seems to be saying that the sexual instinct – *volupté*, even – is shared between all animals, whether human or not. *Girl with a Dog* is a scene of reciprocal adoration and erotic enjoyment.

I have chosen this painting to introduce this book because it is a scene of mutuality between a girl and a dog. To be frank, most of this book is about disharmony, so I wanted readers to be reminded of the carnal joys of truly loving animals. As we all know, people have a poor track record in expressing love for other creatures. We admire exotic wildlife while destroying its habitats. We are distressed by the unkind treatment of animals but regulate their slaughter within abattoirs. Western lifestyles are wholly dependent upon farming animals, which involves practices of extraordinary cruelty. The philosopher Jacques Derrida invented a term to describe human–animal relationships:

'carno-phallogocentrism'. In other words, our treatment of animals is based on privileging masculine traits ('phallo') and the possession of language ('logos'); it involves a willingness to kill and eat other sentient beings ('carno').[1]

But this is not to deny that many of us sincerely love 'our' animals. We call them 'pets'. In fact, pet ownership probably goes back to Palaeolithic times.[2] In 2017–18, 68 per cent of American residences sheltered a pet: that is nearly 85 million homes.[3] In the UK the pet population is around 51 million; 45 per cent of people 'own' one.[4] The most common companion species is dogs, followed by cats. Although pet owners are reluctant to allow their animals to act according to their nature, and many even euthanize them when they become disobedient, unattractive or old, there is general agreement that love for pets means giving them food and water, ensuring they get exercise and talking to them. Half of all pets in the U.S. sleep in the same bed as a member of the human family.[5] We maintain fictive kin relationships with them. There are even websites hosted by 'pet and people wedding specialists' to facilitate human–pet marriages.[6] 'Pets Я Us'. We indulge them, buy them presents, give them names and look upon them as 'almost human'.[7] We kiss and caress them. We dance with them on our beds.

What we don't do is have sex with them. At least, most of us don't. Sex with animals is one of the last taboos, the final bastion of human exceptionalism. The prohibition of what is sometimes called 'bestiality' distinguishes the human subject from the animal object.

Taboo

Why is sex with animals such a taboo? While all other arguments about human exceptionalism have been dismantled, bestiality remains off-limits. It is only in very recent years that some people have begun to undermine the absolute prohibition on zoosexuality.

Are their arguments dangerous, perverted or simply wrongheaded? Or are we entering a new and more amorous phase in human–animal relations? And what does it mean to love non-human animals? More pertinently: what does it mean to love?

This book explores the modern history of human sexual encounters with other species. How have British and American commentators talked about sex with animals and what changing meanings have been attached to the words 'bestiality' and 'zoophilia'? I am curious about debates concerning whether people who are sexually attracted to non-human animals are psychiatrically ill. Do they have a 'paraphilia', a psychiatric term combining the Greek prefix 'para' meaning 'besides' with 'philia' meaning 'love'? Or are they just normal people who happen to have a minority sexual orientation? Given the fraught debates about consent in human-on-human sexual encounters, it is worth asking whether non-human animals can ever consent to libidinal relations with humans. Clearly, sexual intercourse between different species is often harmful; many critics argue it is abusive by definition. I do not agree. This is not to justify bestiality. After all, just because something is not inherently violent or harmful does not mean it is acceptable. This book maintains that we need to think carefully about what we mean when we use complex concepts like 'sex' and 'consent'. This is partly why I believe that exploring human–animal love can help us reflect on love between humans. An ethics of animal-loving can contribute to debates about human, as well as non-human, desires.

I am no fan of arguments based on human exceptionalism. The fundamental premise of this book is that bestiality is not an affront to the 'dignity of man'; neither does it degrade people 'below the level of animals', as Immanuel Kant decreed.[8] The philosopher Peter Morriss even argues that bestiality is regarded by many people as distasteful 'not because it *degrades* animals, but because it *upgrades* them – it treats them as something *better* than they are'. He observes that

Sexual intercourse is supposed to be a sign of love; it is supposed to be carried out between two creatures of approximately equal standing. For a human to have sexual intercourse with an animal implies that it is of equal standing to the human. It denies a hierarchy in which animals are always lower than humans. So it blurs, or denies, boundaries, particularly the boundary between the human and the animal.[9]

In contrast, I see no problem in 'upgrading' non-human animals. Kant believed that humans possess an inherent dignity,[10] but I suggest that non-human animals do as well. Indeed, non-human animals possess inviolable rights to have their interests and preferences respected. They do not exist to serve human ends. Their lives matter to them, as ours do to us.

Definitions

Anyone thinking about this topic is forced to address three definitional conundrums. First, who is the animal? In this book, I often distinguish between humans and animals. Strictly speaking, this is wrong. After all, *Homo sapiens* are as much animals as are *Canis lupus familiaris* (domestic dogs). The term 'animal' has no meaning except 'not human'. In addition, there are innumerable varieties of non-human animals; the cultures of arachnids, apes, dolphins and dingoes are incommensurable. As Derrida reminds us, 'the animal' is nothing more than 'a word that men have given themselves the right to give . . . They have given themselves the word in order to corral a large number of living beings within a single concept: "the Animal", they say.'[11] Employing scientific classifications of species does not help. Scientific disagreements abound; in the biological literature, there are between 9 and 22 definitions of species.[12] Even the species *Homo sapiens* is indeterminate. In the words of the bioethicists Jason Scott Robert and Françoise Baylis, despite all the recent advances in biotechnology, 'the unique identity of the human species cannot be established through genetic or genomic means.'[13]

While admitting to these challenges, in this book I will nevertheless be referring to 'humans' and 'animals' as a convenient shorthand for more complex realities. Occasionally I will write 'non-human animals' in an attempt to draw attention to the fact that humans are also animals. Furthermore, the animals of choice in my analysis will be humans and dogs, although other companion species will appear, most notably cats, horses and dolphins. Whenever possible, the non-human animals referred to in this book will have names. After all, nearly all people give names to their companion species. Even René Descartes, the seventeenth-century French philosopher who was famous for his view that animals were mere automata or moving machines, relented when face-to-face with his much-loved dog, on whom he bestowed the name 'Monsieur Grat'.[14]

When writing about sexual encounters between humans and animals, we are also faced with a proliferation of terms. This is the second definitional problem. Some commentators focus on the act of intercourse: their terms include 'bestiality', 'an unnatural offence', 'buggery', 'sodomy', 'Egyptian', 'animal love' and 'animal sexual abuse'. In contrast, others prefer to assign an identity to human practitioners: they are 'bestialists', 'sodomists', 'zoosexuals' or 'zoos', for example. Psychiatrists have coined a vast number of diagnoses, each seeking to describe distinctive sexual practices or orientations. These include zoophilia, zoophilism, zooerasty, zoostuprum, zoofetishism, zooerastia, zoosadism, formicophilia, animal fetishism and bestiosexuality. While these terms prioritize pathological or medical discourses, my preferred phrase – 'sexual activities between humans and animals' – is not only clumsy but overlooks the fact that sex between humans is also sex between animals. My compromise is to use the terms most appropriate to the time period being addressed as well as the legal, medical and communal contexts of the people

I am writing about. Most commonly, then, I will be writing about bestiality/bestialists, zoophilia/zoophiles and zoosexuals.

Again, this shorthand must not conceal the fact that there is a vast range of activities that take place under bestial or zoophilic labels. In 2011 the *Journal of Forensic and Legal Medicine* published an article by Anil Aggrawal of the Maulana Azad Medical College in New Delhi. He identified ten different categories of zoophiles, ranging from people who simply enjoy animal role-play to those who can be sexually aroused only by engaging in sexual intercourse with animals. Between these two extremes, Aggrawal distinguished between zoophiles who are fantasists, fetishists, sadists and homicidal bestialists. Other zoophiles prefer only tactile encounters or are opportunistic in their sexual choices. Rather problematically, Aggrawal calls people who do not have sex with animals but receive psychosexual satisfaction from them 'romantics'. The implication is that getting 'down and dirty' is incompatible with romance. For Aggrawal, 'regular' or 'classic' zoosexuals are those who enjoy sex with both humans and animals.[15]

Even Aggrawal's ten-point classification system fails to encompass the vast variety of practices and desires awash in zoosexual worlds. To his classification system could be added zoophilic voyeurism, frotteurism (rubbing against animals) and necrozoophilia (sexual attraction to dead animals). It could also be expanded to include a range of terms based on a desire for different animal partners. To take just five examples, these include aelurophilia, canophilia, musophilia, ornithophilia and anolingis, which refer (respectively) to being aroused by cats, dogs, mice, birds and the act of licking lizards. There are even Latinate terms for specific sadistic encounters: avisodomists, for example, are men who penetrate the cloacas of birds, breaking their necks immediately prior to ejaculation.[16]

The third and final question that needs to be discussed is: what is sex? Humans engage in a range of activities we call 'sexual', including caressing, kissing, masturbating, cunnilinging, fellating and penetrating the anus or vagina, to name just a few. As we shall see, both in legal texts and animal protection discourses, the assumption is often made that 'bestiality' involves penetration of the mouth, anus or vagina of one or more of the participants. This makes it easier to argue that the acts are offensive because of potential or actual injury. Ethical issues become less clear-cut if 'sexual' includes non-penetrative eroticism or non-genital sensuality, such as when a woman is aroused by ants collecting honey from her hand or mons pubis (as in formicophilia) or when a cat licks a woman's vulva. It is no coincidence that these two examples involve sexual acts between women and animals, since female sexualities are routinely assumed to be less aggressive than their male counterparts. As we shall see, debates about bestiality have too often assumed a phallic model of sexuality that de-eroticizes most of the body, localizing sexual pleasure in the human or animal penis.

Prevalence

Imprecision in defining the main terms is compounded by the almost total absence of reliable statistical information about how many people engage in sexual activities with animals. Many psychiatrists, physicians and social workers are too embarrassed to report incidents.[17] Even lawmakers are reluctant to mention it. Attempts to criminalize bestiality in Pennsylvania and Florida, for example, were delayed because legislators were loath to discuss the topic: 'It is yucky,' noted one.[18] This disgust factor makes bestialists profoundly aware of the need for secrecy. Admitting to having sex with animals carries a huge stigma. Even men convicted of sex offences against humans are reluctant to admit to being sexually aroused by animals. In one 2014 study 38 per cent of juvenile male sex offenders confessed to having had sexual intercourse with an animal; when these young men were asked the same question using a polygraph lie detector test, the percentage soared to 81 per cent.[19] Zoophiles routinely find themselves socially and legally ostracized.[20] They may even be wary of fellow zoophiles. In one Internet survey, for instance, more than 40 per cent of zoophiles were reluctant to meet others in person 'since they regarded them as "weird"'.[21] In other words, the stigma had been internalized.

Reliable data is also hampered by the fact that bestiality is not generally witnessed. Most acts take place in private. The tiny proportion of legal cases that lead to arrests and convictions are often folded into statistics that refer to 'buggery' between consenting male homosexuals. As discussed in Chapter Four, many of the surveys of bestiality are undertaken in psychiatric or penal settings, making them highly skewed towards deviant populations who indulge in extreme practices such as zoosadism. This means that the high correlation between men who practise bestiality and go on to hurt other people may be due, in fact, to sample bias. In contrast, surveys of self-confessed zoophiles go to the other extreme. They are often based on men and women who have joined specialist, community-based Internet chatrooms; respondents tend to be computer-savvy men who are keen to make a positive impression in order to reduce hatred levelled against their communities.

Nor do we know much about the animals involved. Studies involving zoophiles show that the most sexually favoured animals are male dogs, followed by female dogs and then male horses. The fourth most favoured animals are female horses (for men) and male cats (for women).[22] However, a vast range of other animals can become sexual companions, including donkeys, goats, pigs, sheep, cows, chickens, turkeys, hamsters, dolphins, eels and octopuses. More unusual preferences include camels, deer, llamas, bulls, boars and gorillas.[23] Although the evidence is not clear-cut, there seems to be a high correlation between human gender orientation (for example, heterosexual versus homosexual) and the zoophile's human gender preference in animals.[24]

The actual number and personal identities of these animals are not known. Only rarely are the animals named. If they are not injured, these animals do not come to the attention of veterinarians and other human carers. Even veterinary surgeons admit it is a taboo subject in their profession; well into the twenty-first century, textbooks on animal obstetrics and gynaecology routinely fail to mention the possibility of sexual interference when treating animals who have suffered vaginal injuries.[25] Animal victims are often subsequently killed, their deaths unmourned.

These are formidable limitations. It has led to a situation where nearly everyone who works in the field cites the American sexologist Alfred C. Kinsey's extraordinary surveys in *Sexual Behavior in the Human Male* (1948) and *Sexual Behavior in the Human Female* (1953). Kinsey and his colleagues (who included the sexologists Wardell B. Pomeroy, Clyde E. Martin and Paul H. Gebhard) found that one adult American male in twelve or fourteen (that is, 8 per cent) claimed to have had a sexual encounter with an animal. In farming communities 17 per cent had experienced orgasm as a result of animal contact since their adolescence, but this statistic rose as high as 65 per cent in some locations. Kinsey concluded:

> Ultimately, 14 to 16 per cent of the rural males of the grade school level, 20 per cent of the rural males of the high school level, and 26 to 28 per cent of the rural males of the college level have had some animal experience to the point of orgasm.

In most cases, the sexual encounter was a passing phase or occurred as substitutes for heterosexual human relationships. Nevertheless, Kinsey admitted that strong emotional ties could develop between farm boys and their animal loves: there were even men who were 'quite upset emotionally, when situations force them to sever connections with the particular animal'.[26]

Kinsey also asked American women about their sexual practices. He thought that females were 'less inclined' than males to be 'aroused by a variety of psychosexual stimuli'. He believed that this was because women were less dependent on 'psychological stimulation'. However, Kinsey did find that just under 4 per cent of American women admitted that, since adolescence, they had engaged in sex with an animal. An even smaller proportion (1.5 per cent) of pre-adolescents had engaged in such acts. Nearly all of these sexual contacts involved pets such as dogs and cats.[27]

The only other major, population-wide survey took place in 1972. The science writer Morton Hunt sampled 2,026 people aged over eighteen years and living in 24 urban areas across the U.S. He found that 5 per cent of American men and 2 per cent of women reported at least one sexual encounter with an animal.[28] His prevalence rate was lower than that of Kinsey because Hunt's sample were more urbanized and therefore had more limited access to animals.

Despite the prominence of Kinsey's and Hunt's surveys, they were not the only ones. Excluding surveys based on psychiatric and prison populations and those dependent on self-confessed zoophiles (which will be discussed in chapters Three and Four, respectively), smaller studies include those of the sexologist Marilyn D. Story. In 1974 and again in 1980, she asked fifty single men and fifty single women taking her sexuality course at the University of Northern Iowa about their sexual practices. In 1974, 11 per cent admitted to having had sexual contact with an animal; this had dropped to 3 per cent by 1980.[29]

The usefulness of all of these surveys is highly questionable. Clearly, young American men and women taking a sexuality course in a university in northern Iowa are hardly representative of the general population. Their increasing caution about admitting to sexual contact with animals was also likely to be affected by societal changes in American society between 1974 and 1980, including the rise of evangelicalism and the conservative Right.

But Kinsey's and Hunt's population-wide surveys are equally problematic. Not only were they based on research conducted between fifty years (Hunt) and three-quarters of a century (Kinsey) ago, but the methodologies employed were flawed. Hunt was neither a trained sociologist nor a sexologist. Kinsey's 'persuasive', even aggressive, interviewing style has often been noted.[30]

Faced with the absence of reliable data, many commentators simply make assertions based on personal impressions, therapeutic orientation and political agenda. Anecdotal reports include claims by sex therapists in the twenty-first century that urban clients are increasingly speaking about engaging in sexual activities with their pets.[31] They speculate that this is due to the isolating effect of Internet use, loneliness and fear of face-to-face intimacy.[32] Other commentators simply make unsubstantiated claims that bestiality is 'not uncommon in some districts and under certain circumstances'.[33] No evidence is provided.

Curiosity

Imprecise definitions and the lack of data on the numbers involved have not inhibited public interest in human–animal sexual practices. In the 1960s NASA even funded a project (designed by the neuroscientist John Cunningham Lilly but led by Gregory Bateson, the influential anthropologist and cyberneticist) that attempted to teach dolphins to speak through their blow holes.[34] Margaret Lovatt was recruited to talk to a dolphin called Peter, living and sleeping with him six days a week in the Dolphin House on the Caribbean island of St Thomas. In later years, Lovatt admitted that Peter was randy and 'would rub himself on my knee, or my foot, or my hand'. In the end Peter's sexual arousals became so disruptive that she simply began to masturbate him regularly. 'I allowed that,' she noted, adding, 'I wasn't uncomfortable with it, as long as it wasn't rough. It would just become part of what was going on, like an itch – just get

rid of it, scratch it and move on.'[35] Unfortunately, the project was
eventually decommissioned, in part because of concerns about the
use of LSD in some of the other experiments. Peter was shipped off
to another tank in Miami and, trapped in a place with little sunshine
and without his beloved Lovatt, it was claimed that he committed
suicide by voluntarily holding his breath.

This project was clearly exceptional. However, it does draw
attention to the fact that, for a practice which is viewed with
abhorrence by many people, even NASA scientists are drawn into
it. Indeed, despite claims that it is a taboo subject, it is remarkable
how often we talk about it. There are numerous books, films, theatre
productions, paintings and photographs whose subject is sex between
different species. Many examples will appear in this book.

It does not take much effort to discover that non-human
animals are central to humanity's sexual imaginary. From the earliest
human cultures onwards, cave paintings and other artistic forms
depict humans having sex with animals. The most ancient evidence
is a Palaeolithic (8000 BC) cave painting in Italy showing a man

Margaret Howe Lovatt at the Dolphin House on St Thomas.

A rock drawing depicting bestiality in Sweden from the Bronze Age.

penetrating an animal. Depictions of such sexual acts abound in the Iron and Bronze Ages as well.[36]

Myths involving human–animal hybrids are common: we have only to think of satyrs (human/goat), centaurs (human/horse) and the Minotaur (human/bull). Some indigenous peoples in Southeast Asia, Australasia and North America tell stories of their ancient ancestry emerging from sexual encounters between women and dogs. In ancient myths gods regularly transmute into animals and seduce humans, who seem incapable of resisting their charms. One of the most popular is the story of Leda and the Swan. When Jupiter falls in love with the beautiful Leda, he conjures up a plot whereby he changes himself into a swan and, after staging an attack by an eagle, gets Leda to rescue him. A particularly erotic depiction of this myth was painted by François Boucher, an eighteenth-century French painter of the highly ornamental Rococo school and one of Fragonard's teachers. Boucher's *Leda and the Swan* (c. 1740) shows the phallic swan's neck moving between her legs. Indeed, male swans are one of the few birds who possess a penis.

However, we do not have to look to highly ornamental art for depictions of bestiality. Stories of animals abducting virginal girls, falling in love and then having children with them date back to ancient times.[37] In the ancient Roman novel *Lucius; or, The Ass*, for example, a young man is transformed into an ass, with whom a woman falls in love. Prior to their wedding, the ass accidentally eats a rose leaf and is miraculously changed into a man again. However, the woman repels him on the grounds that he no longer possesses the large sexual organs of a donkey.[38] Similarly, in early modern Britain readers delighted in satires depicting nymphomaniac women who used animals to satisfy their desires. One example is the heroine of John Marston's book *The Scourge of Villanie* (1598), who took a donkey as a lover. Eighteenth-century literature regularly introduced the trope of a male dog becoming a sexual rival to a male human

François Boucher, *Leda and the Swan*, c. 1740, oil on canvas.

lover.[39] In Alexander Pope's mock-heroic poem *The Rape of the Lock*, he notes that the two crises of a woman's life were 'when husbands die, or lapdogs breathe their last'. In a snide joke, he observed that Belinda's lap-dog 'wak'd his mistress with his tongue'.[40] Folktales, too, dwell lovingly on pretty young girls who, after being shipwrecked on a people-free island, are forced to become lovers to the 'boss of the monkeys' or another 'baboon fellow'. These tales invariably end badly. In one Irish example, the monkey-lover and his human wife have three children together and are described as 'getting on fine' – that is, until she is rescued by the crew of another ship. As soon as she leaves, 'the boso [sic] monkey . . . caught the three children and he got a knife, and he cut the heads off the three of them.'[41] Thankfully, children's books are replete with stories of more affectionate animal husbands, such as Frog Princes, and the Beauties and Beasts who kiss and fall asleep in each other's arms.

The popularity of bestiality in the arts has not declined in modern times – indeed, it has arguably increased. Sexual relations between species appear in literature such as Sir Richard Francis Burton's translation of *The Book of the Thousand Nights and a Night* (1885), as well as H. G. Wells's *The Island of Dr Moreau* (1896) and its film version, *Island of Lost Souls* (1932). Theatrical audiences have been treated to productions of Bamber Gascoigne's *Leda Had a Little Swan* of 1964 and A. R. Gurney's *Sylvia* of 1995.[42] In *Everything You Always Wanted to Know about Sex (But Were Afraid to Ask)* (1972), Woody Allen includes a character who is in love with his sheep. When he confesses his desire to his psychiatrist, there is a moment of disgust – until the psychiatrist also falls in love with the sheep. Zoophilia is regularly the source of comedy.[43]

Modern films and theatre performances are much more likely than their predecessors to address the question of emotional, as well as erotic, love between individuals of different species. This is the theme of Nagisa Oshima's *Max, mon amour* (1986), which portrays the lives of British diplomat Peter Jones (Anthony Higgins) and his wife

Margaret (Charlotte Rampling), son Nelson (Christopher Hovik) and maid Maria (Victoria Abril). Margaret takes a lover whom Peter discovers to be a chimpanzee. In one discussion, Peter asks a zoologist at dinner whether love between a monkey and a woman is possible: 'I'm not talking about sex. I'm talking about love . . . Is love possible only between members of the same species? Could a horse fall in love with a snake?' In an interview talking about this film, the actress Rampling admitted:

> I'm not shocked easily, but I was shocked . . . The shocking thing was the element of – you could say – bestiality. And I'd say it was about that . . . in a way . . . perhaps breaking that taboo . . . the actual sexuality of the film is non-existent and all-existent, because sexuality is in everything.[44]

Ironically, the person inside the monkey suit was the actress Aisla Berk, not a man – making it even more perverse.

The question of interspecies love is even more prominent in Edward Albee's *The Goat; or, Who Is Sylvia?* (2000). In Albee's play it is the husband, Martin, who falls in love – this time with a goat

Gene Wilder, as Dr Doug Ross, and Daisy in *Everything You Always Wanted to Know about Sex (But Were Afraid to Ask)* (1972, dir. Woody Allen).

Charrlotte Rampling in *Max, mon amour* (1986, dir. Nagisa Oshima).

called Sylvia. Martin's wife, Stevie, is angry: she feels humiliated and polluted. Martin is keen to reassure Stevie that Sylvia is female. Stevie's response is a scream: 'So long as it's female, eh? So long as it's got a cunt it's all right with you!' Martin yells back, 'A SOUL!! Don't you know the difference!? Not a cunt, a soul!' Stevie then whimpers, 'You can't fuck a soul!', to which Martin responds, 'No, and it isn't about fucking.'

None of these art forms can match the influence of *King Kong* on the bestial imagination. Critics and audiences have read the different versions of the film in many ways, pointing out its racism (especially its depictions of the dangers of miscegenation), its facile gender stereotypes and its commentary on the risks inherent in releasing primitive sexual drives.[45] But there is also the power of love and erotic desire, as in the 1933 version of the film when Kong removes Ann's clothes and delicately sniffs her. This acknowledgement of beastly sensuality was stripped from Peter Jackson's 2005 version,

Jessica Lange in *King Kong* (1976, dir. John Guillermin).

in which Ann is instead seen performing a song-and-dance routine in a parody of romantic love.

Our infatuation with images and creative literature depicting sex between humans and animals suggests the degree to which animal and human sexuality are interwoven into human life and culture. Our entanglements with non-human others go deep into our culture – our psyches, even.

Dissent and Queerness

Although literature and art have never been shy about human–animal sexual relations, the same is not the case in non-fiction and social scientific literature. There, bestiality remains a taboo. The extent of the distaste for the topic was publicly revealed in 2001 when Peter Singer, the prominent ethicist and animal liberationist, reviewed a new edition of Midas Dekkers's 1994 book *Dearest Pet*, which is still the only modern book-length discussion of bestial imaginaries and practices. Singer's review came out in 2001 in the relatively obscure online magazine *Nerve*, which focuses on sex and relationships. Singer was probably not expecting it to generate the reprobation that it did, which was largely because he seemed to be defending the practice of having sex with consenting animals. Singer contended that the 'taboo on sex with animals' probably 'originated as part of a broader rejection of non-reproductive sex'. However, he continued,

> the vehemence with which this prohibition continues to be held, its persistence while other non-reproductive sexual acts have become acceptable, suggests that there is another powerful force at work: our desire to differentiate ourselves, erotically and in every other way, from animals.[46]

Singer had clearly hit a raw nerve, upsetting a great many of his friends as well as an army of detractors. In particular he was criticized for objectifying women as well as non-human animals. Surely it wasn't necessary to use phrases such as 'a giant octopus who appears to be sucking her cunt' and 'a man fucking a large quadruped of indeterminate species'? Feminists criticized him for legitimating 'the use of non-humans for pornographic gratification' and for forgetting that such acts were 'a symptom of the broader societal attitude that domination is acceptable'.[47] Some of Singer's fans among the animal liberationist and rights movements called for him to be 'exiled from the modern movement' or at least to step down as head of the Great Ape Project.[48] At the very least, he was censured for discrediting pro-animal movements by publishing such a 'shameless essay'.[49] The *Wall Street Journal* declared that Singer's defence of bestiality would 'come as a tremendous embarrassment to professional ethicists'.[50] The *Village Voice* called him the worst name they could think of: 'You're an Animal,' ran the headline.[51] To which Singer would have answered, 'Well, yes.'

The angry responses to Singer's article suggest that, in 2001 at least, people were not ready for a frank and measured debate about expressions of sexual love between species. His article also illustrates the profoundly sexist attitudes of many commentators, as we shall see throughout this book.

HOWEVER, much has changed in the two decades since Singer penned his review of *Dearest Pet*. In particular, queer sexualities have come to wider public knowledge, along with queer theorizing. I have been both challenged and inspired by such work. This is why this book embraces a post-humanist discourse that acknowledges the embodiment and embeddedness of the animal in the world. I will be suggesting that animals are actors in society. This serves to challenge the anthropocentrism of history, human exceptionalism and the idea that culture is an entirely human preserve. Although we can never truly know the Other, I believe that we can make sensible deductions about it. This book, therefore, is a contribution to a new turn in animal studies away from rights speak and towards rites, performativity, hybridity, interrelatedness and queerness.

One

The Law

Define: **Criminal**.
c. 1400, 'sinful, wicked'; mid-C15, 'of or pertaining to a legally punishable offence; late-C15, 'guilty of a crime', from Old French *criminel*, 'criminal, despicable, wicked'.

Enumclaw is a small city near Seattle in southeast Washington State. According to the indigenous Salish peoples, its name translates as 'a place of evil spirits', although locals prefer to claim it means 'thundering noise'.[1] Based in the middle of flat farmlands and dairy farms, Enumclaw is a place where horses are both admired and loved.

Late on the evening of 1 July 2005, on a farm just 8 km (5 mi.) northwest of Enumclaw, 45-year-old Boeing engineer and doting father Kenneth Pinyan was anally penetrated by a stallion known colloquially as 'Big Dick'. Early the following morning, a friend – subsequently identified as James Michael Tait – dumped his pulseless body at the community hospital. Pinyan died of acute peritonitis due to a perforated colon.

An article detailing the sordid events and published in the *Seattle Weekly* was the paper's most read article of 2005 and the four follow-up stories were all in the top twenty.[2] The locals were aghast. As details emerged, however, they turned angry. It quickly became clear that Pinyan's sexual proclivities were not unique to him. Quite a few men with bestial cravings had visited Tait's farm: indeed, there were hundreds of hours of videotape recordings documenting their bacchanalian activities. One of these tapes showed Pinyan's final encounter with Big Dick. For a city proud of loving horses, Pinyan had 'brought a bad light to the close relationship many [residents] had with their animals'.[3]

The fact that these bestial encounters were not illegal further enraged commentators. State laws made the physical abuse of animals a criminal offence, but none of the animals on the farm or on the videotapes seemed to have been harmed. The only crime that Tait could be charged with was trespass. He lived in a trailer parked next to a farm that bred Arabian stallions. Most of the sex recorded in the videotapes had taken place on Tait's property, but on the night Pinyan died Tait's horse had refused to perform. This led Tait, Pinyan and a third man who was not publicly identified to sneak into a neighbour's barn without the owner's knowledge. Tait was eventually given a one-year suspended sentence, ordered to pay a fine of $300, forbidden to have contact with his neighbours and required to perform eight hours of community service.

State politicians wanted to ensure that they could punish people like Tait more harshly in the future. They discovered that bestiality used to be illegal in Washington State under anti-sodomy laws. The decriminalization of consensual sodomy (that is, male homosexual acts) in 1976 had inadvertently also decriminalized bestiality.[4] In addition, they found, bestiality was already a felony offence in seven states and a misdemeanour in around two dozen other states. In South Dakota convicted bestialists had to register as sex offenders.[5]

The Republican State Senator Pam Roach decided that action was needed. By introducing Senate Bill 6417, aimed at making bestiality a Class C felony, Roach led the move to criminalize bestiality in Washington State. On 1 February 2006 the state's Senate voted unanimously to make bestiality a crime, although some senators would not actually sign the Bill because they found the idea of bestiality too 'repugnant' to even think about.[6] The law meant that people prosecuted for the offence could be punished with up to five years in a state prison and/or a $10,000 fine.

In the process of drafting the legislation, however, there had been unforeseen complications. The most important one was how to differentiate bestiality from normal animal husbandry practices. This was important since Washington State was heavily dependent on the farming of animals. Dairy farmers had routinely used artificial insemination since the 1950s; pig farmers had been artificially inseminating swine from the 1990s.[7] As we will see, the only thing differentiating bestiality from the manipulation of sexual organs as part of farm animal and thoroughbred reproduction was the motivation of the human participant: one was libidinal, the other economic. Senator Roach had the unenviable task of trying to explain why artificial insemination was 'an act of [animal] husbandry' that was 'different' from bestiality.[8] The final wording of the Act was intended to ensure that the distinction was kept. The law decreed that a person would be guilty of animal cruelty if she or he 'knowingly engage[d] in any sexual conduct or sexual contact with an animal' or aided, observed, organized, promoted, advertised or filmed such acts. Crucially, the law outlawed human–animal sexual contact only when it was 'for the purpose of sexual gratification or arousal of the person'.[9] On these points, conservatives, animal rights advocates, sex assault victims, dairymen, poultry producers and children's advocates agreed. The law came into force on 7 June 2006.

Laws such as the one implemented after the death of Pinyan represented a new, punitive attitude towards people who did not visibly injure animals but nevertheless had sex with them. What reasons did Washingtonians give for passing such a law? Explanations ranged from the pragmatic to the philosophical. Roach was astonished to discover that Washington was 'one of the few states in the country that doesn't outlaw this activity . . . This has made Washington a Mecca for bestiality. People know it isn't against the law and so they come from other states to have sex with animals.'[10]

Like other commentators, she appealed to anxieties about perverted, urban 'outsiders' who were polluting Washington's more 'natural' rural communities. In particular, long-standing regional differences were mentioned, including the fear that eastern parts of the state were being tainted by influences from the less respectable, more permissive urban regions in the west. The journalist Doug Clark alluded to the 'inferiority complex' of 'my fellow Eastern Washingtonians' when faced with the 'so-called cultural superiority of the West Side'.[11] In an article written in the *Spokesman Review*, Clark even addressed Pam Roach directly, insisting that the whole debate about bestiality was really 'A West Side problem'. 'Don't try to rope us into this mess, Pam,' he contended, adding: 'I shudder to imagine what kind of wild weed they're grazing on west of the Cascades. But we Eastern Washingtonians have enough horse sense to know the difference between loving our pets and "loving" our pets.'[12]

This emphasis on territorial variations overlapped with another anxiety that was its exact opposite: de-territorialization. The Internet was blamed for perverting morality. Deviants were no longer isolated individuals but could form online communities, thereby supporting each other while at the same time spreading their vices to unsuspecting novices. This was particularly worrying because anti-bestiality commentators were convinced that people who abused animals would also abuse humans: bestial acts were a slippery slope to all-too-human violence.[13] Roach, for example, took it as axiomatic that 'abusers develop by starting with something helpless, an animal; next is a child. There are patterns that develop.'[14] Statistics bolstering this claim were plucked out of thin air. Dan Satterberg of the King County Prosecutor's Office even asserted that sex with animals inevitably leads to aggression towards people, claiming that an astonishing 96 per cent of juvenile sex offenders 'started off abusing the family pet'.[15]

A more principled approach was taken by anti-vice campaigners who focused on the inability of animals to consent to sexual activity with humans. This was the most common explanation for why a legal ban was required. It was summed up succinctly by Roach when she noted, 'It's really a bill that will protect animals, who are innocent, by the fact that they can't consent.'[16] Just as children could not consent to sexual activity (in Roach's words, 'children do not consent; children are innocent'), neither could animals ('they're innocent'), meaning that sex with either was a form of sexual abuse.[17] This was why the *Seattle Post-Intelligencer* believed that 'It should be a no-brainer that animal cruelty laws ought to cover sex acts.'[18]

Finally, lurking behind many of the justifications for a ban on non-injurious bestial practices was human exceptionalism. This argument was forcefully made by Wesley J. Smith of the Discovery Institute, a think tank that advocates (among other things) the teaching of intelligent design. In an article entitled 'Horse Sense', published in the conservative *Weekly Standard* on 30 August 2005, Smith argued that bestiality was 'profoundly degrading and utterly subversive to the crucial understanding that human beings are unique, special, and of the highest moral worth in the known universe – a concept known as "human exceptionalism".'[19]

Indeed, Smith exemplifies the tension between two very different anti-bestiality activists: right-wing moralists and animal-rights liberals. The alliance between these two groups over animal protection was severely strained when spokesmen like Smith combined his anti-bestiality rhetoric with attacks on the animal rights organization People for the Ethical Treatment of Animals (PETA). Smith lambasted PETA for basing their ethics on the ability of animals to feel pain, claiming that their opposition to cattle farming on the grounds that it was 'as evil as human slavery' was ridiculous.[20] Smith also condemned the 'bioethics movement' for failing to recognize that humans 'have a special value'; for him, PETA's slogan 'We are all animals' was 'espousing an explicit moral equality between man and beasts'.[21]

These tensions might have been relegated to a footnote in the history of Washington State if the manner of Pinyan's death had not become a national discussion point. This was largely due to the release of a film entitled *Zoo*. Although originally the film was called *In the Forest There Is Every Kind of Bird*, it was part-documentary and part-reconstruction of the events at Enumclaw. Directed by Robinson Devor, it premiered at the Sundance Film Festival in January 2007, where it was one of sixteen winners out of 856 candidates. Devor claimed to be breaking 'the last taboo'.[22] It is a beautifully constructed film that also engages with difficult questions about human–animal relations, the politics of animal protection and zoophilic desires. Some of the main protagonists are interviewed in the film, including Pam Roach, 'Coyote', 'Mr H.' (a ranch hand) and the 'Happy Horse-man' (whose real name was Mark Matthews; I discuss him at the start of Chapter Four). Only Jenny Edwards (a self-proclaimed horse rescuer), her husband, John, and 'Coyote' agreed to appear on screen. 'Mr Hands' (that is, the deceased Pinyan) and the other zoos were played by actors. The film asks important questions but, most notably, it makes audiences think about whether or not animals can actually give consent. Devor believed that there was 'some love in this story – some beauty and friendship and emotion'.[23] Not surprisingly, he was accused of 'over-aestheticizing' bestiality, even though the film does include some incredibly blunt statements, including one comment by a zoo admitting that 'Maybe I just want to grab a horse by its nuts, feel his balls, how they feel – well, yeah, they're warm.'

The most poignant segment of the film is the encounter between the stallion Pinyan had sex with (whose name was Strut, but Pinyan and his friends dubbed him 'Big Dick') and Jenny Edwards, whose love for horses had been bolstered during long nights she spent with them in her attempts to come to terms with a cancer diagnosis. In the film, audiences are informed that Tait had been looking after Strut but, after Pinyan's death, Pinyan's brother and Jenny

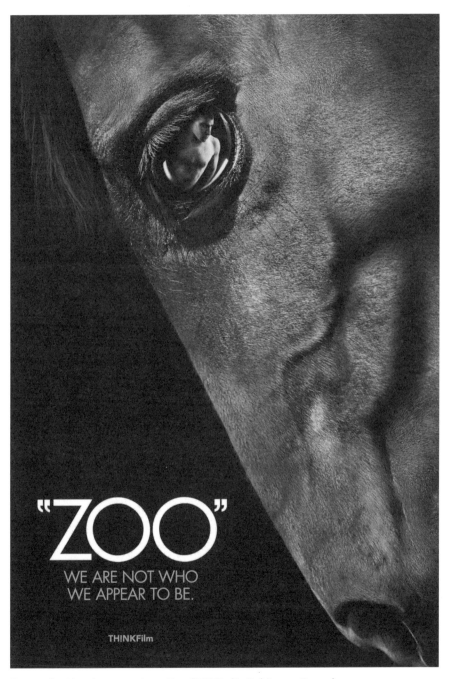

Poster for the documentary *Zoo* (2007, dir. Robinson Devor).

Edwards decided to remove Strut from Tait's unhealthy influence. In an unscripted moment in the film, when Edwards is leading Strut towards the trailer, an unnamed small pony canters into view and begins to fellate the stallion. For Edwards, this was proof that the horse had become as corrupt and 'bestial' as the zoophiles. She decided to restore Strut's innocence by castrating him. In a shocking sequence, audiences witness Strut being anaesthetized and hung in an operating room, and having his testicles removed. Ironically, the film identifies the animal rescuer as the human who inflicts the most damage upon the horse.

Perhaps just as shocking as the *Zoo* documentary, however, is the realization that not everyone was saddened by the fates of Pinyan and Strut. A thirty-second porn video called *2 Guys 1 Horse* can be found on the Internet: it is the actual amateur video of Strut penetrating Pinyan, shot shortly before he died.[24] In other words, it is a snuff film. In addition, despite the fact that a man was killed and a stallion castrated as the result of some fairly straightforward sexual encounters, many people found the incident hilarious. The journalist Doug Clark, for example, can be heard singing a funny song about the tragedies. The song's upbeat lyrics, with animal noises and circus-like music, included the lines:

> A man and a horse
> Had intercourse!
> The force of the horse
> Made the dude a corpse!
> You can't do that with a horse, of course.
> It's BEST-IAL-ITY![25]

Equally tactless, Comedy Central's *Broad City* aired an episode in its third series entitled 'Game's Over', in which Ilana Wexler (played by Ilana Glazer), attempting to advertise a discount on colonics, retweets a video of a man being penetrated by a horse. While her co-workers grimace, groan and vomit, Wexler's boss berates her for circulating a video 'of a guy fucking a horse'. Ilana responds by quipping, 'If you did your homework . . . you would know that the *horse* was fucking the *guy*. It's chill.' The notion that consent can be assumed if the male animal is the one doing the penetration seemed obviously correct to some commentators. As right-wing radio host Rush Limbaugh asked, 'How the hell do we know that the horse didn't consent? Can this happen without consent? . . . If the horse didn't consent, then none of this would have happened.'[26] It is an argument that has been used to claim that if a boy or man gets an erection during a sexual assault, they must have been a willing participant.

Outlawing Bestiality

In the U.S. the Enumclaw tragedy was one of the most widely discussed instances of bestial harm and led to a wave of legislation that criminalized human–animal sexual conduct, irrespective of harm to the animal. It was not unique, however. A similar incident happened in Arizona the following year (2006) – although that time no one actually died. In that case, Leroy Johnson (the former deputy fire chief at the city of Mesa fire department) was caught with his trousers down, lying on top of a small grey lamb. Although his intentions were obvious, he had been too intoxicated to complete the act.[27] As in Washington, there was widespread dismay by Arizonians that bestiality was not a crime in their state. All that Johnson could be charged with was a misdemeanour. He pleaded guilty to disorderly conduct and was sentenced to eighteen months' probation. During that period, he was barred from owning any animals (although an exception was made for his dog Major and two turtles), had to abstain from drinking and was required to see a counsellor. A local newspaper, called the *Smoking Gun*, thought Johnson had gotten off too lightly. It got its revenge by publishing

Johnson's mug shot as well as a photograph of his 'young victim'. Within a couple of months bestiality had also been criminalized in Arizona.[28] In 2017, 42 states had enacted anti-bestiality laws or other laws against the sexual abuse of animals. Kansas, Michigan and Mississippi did so under sodomy statutes, while Montana banned deviant sexual conduct with animals in the same statute that banned deviant sexual conduct between people of the same sex. Only eight states and Washington, DC, did not have bestiality laws – Kentucky, Hawaii, Nevada, New Mexico, Texas, Vermont, West Virginia and Wyoming – although Kentucky was considering an anti-bestiality law that would apply only to dogs and cats.[29]

Why might the law wish to criminalize bestial acts? Clearly the main reason is that sexual acts between humans and animals are usually abusive: they often harm the animal and regularly occur without consent. These problems will be explored in greater depth in the next chapter. But there were many other reasons, including religious moralism, historical tradition and the harm done to humans. As I will argue, the first two explanations form the bedrock of prohibitions on bestiality but they cannot explain why human–animal sexual relations were decriminalized in some periods of history, nor why they were later recriminalized. To understand those trends, we need to understand not only the rise of animal rights (which is the theme of the next chapter) but the rise of human rights, with its increased concern for human well-being.

Church and State

Entrenched religious prohibitions have not only governed attitudes towards human–animal sexual intercourse, but informed the law. Like other forms of non-reproductive sex, such as homosexuality and queer sex, human–animal intercourse has been universally condemned by religious leaders. Judeo-Christian texts denounce bestiality as a major sin. Leviticus 18:22–4 states that humans 'defile' themselves when they 'lie with any beast'. 'It is a confusion,' the scriptures contend. Leviticus 20:15–16 reiterates the point, insisting that a man or woman who has sexual intercourse with any beast 'shall surely be put to death: and ye shall slay the beast'. Similar verses can be found in Deuteronomy 27:21 and Exodus 22:19.

Despite widespread secularization, religious authorities remain at the forefront of arguments against bestiality. In the 1980s, for example, an elder in the Free Church of Scotland warned that bestiality was 'rife in Sutherland' (and perhaps he should know since he was a shepherd as well as a church elder); he contended that this was a disturbing example of the 'work of the devil'.[30] The resurgence of evangelicalism and the religious right in the U.S. has also seen a revival of concern about this 'abhorrent vice'. Today, the 'damnable practice' continues to be condemned from pulpits throughout the world.

These theological prohibitions are policed by the law. The criminalization of bestiality has a very long, entrenched history. This book focuses on the period from the nineteenth century to the present, with a particular emphasis on British and American practices. However, there is a sophisticated and growing literature on bestiality in earlier times, including scholarship on the Middle Ages and the early modern period.[31] One of the most prominent researchers in the field is the historian Jonas Liliequist, who explores seventeenth- and eighteenth-century Sweden. He found that by 1778, when the last person was beheaded and burned at the stake for bestiality, between six and seven hundred people had been executed for the crime in Sweden.[32] Bestiality prosecutions at this time accounted for between 25 and 35 per cent of all executions. Indeed, throughout Europe, prosecutions for bestiality were more common than those for sodomy or male-on-male sex.[33] An unknown number of bestialists were punished in other ways, such as being driven from the community, forced to perform public labour in chains and flogged. Along with infanticide, bestiality was regarded as one of the most heinous crimes.

In attempting to explain this phenomenon, Liliequist argues that it is not enough to point to the increased power of the Church and state, together with more effective policing of village life, although these did have some influence. It can also not be fully explained in terms of sexual frustration, a consequence of the rise in the average age of marriage combined with religious as well as legal sanctions against sex outside of wedlock. Rather, Liliequist points to 'the underlying cultural meaning of bestiality as a transgressional act – transgression of the culturally constructed boundaries between man and animal, between male and female, between men and boys'.[34] This was why those who merely witnessed bestial acts were also thought to have endangered their souls by risking God's wrath.[35]

A less dramatic picture emerges when we turn to Britain. Historically, bestiality was subsumed under legislation prohibiting 'buggery', or non-reproductive sex. No distinction was made between buggery between two men and between a man and an animal. However, prior to the sixteenth century, the crime of buggery was not harshly punished. This changed in 1533 with the passing of the Buggery Act, which outlawed the 'detestable and abominable Vice of Buggery committed with mankind or beast'. 'Bestial' acts were so offensive that the penalty was death. This remained the case when the laws were reformed in 1828 under the Offences against the Person Act. The ultimate penalty was removed only in 1861, when imprisonment became the main way of punishing offenders, although the number of years served varied from a few months to life.

Throughout this period, though, relatively few cases of bestiality were prosecuted. From 1674 to 1834, only eleven cases appeared before the Old Bailey.[36] As in Sweden, bestiality was primarily a rural vice.[37] It was viewed as a disruption of the God-ordained order that placed humans at the top of the hierarchy of beings, as well as being linked to theological anxieties, such as fears that demons were fond of appearing before humans in animal disguises, and concerns about the pollution of species.[38] Bestial acts were regarded as just as much of a sin as homosexuality and masturbation and therefore could be more harshly punished if committed by a married, as opposed to a single, man.

Offenders in Britain also tended to be treated more leniently than in Sweden. In 1734, for instance, eleven-year-old Jeffrey Skuse, who had been caught with his penis 'fasten'd' to a dog, was let off. The court record states that 'on account of his Youth the court tho't to shown him Compassion'.[39] If age was one factor that could be taken into consideration, intelligence was another. In 1758 a Royal Marine who had been convicted of 'buggery upon the body of a she-goat' was described in court as an 'illiterate, ignorant, stupid young fellow'; he was 'deprived of all natural capacity and next to an idiot'.[40] The king pardoned him.

Importantly, animals who incited the passions of humans were not necessarily considered innocent. After all, while the Royal Marine was pardoned by the king on the grounds that he was an 'idiot', the goat was ignobly executed. It was seen as relevant that the animal responded to human advances and therefore was not a passive victim or an object of human lust. This helps explain why there were strong taboos associated with animals who had been sexually active with humans: they could not be eaten, for example, nor could their milk be drunk. Sometimes this was because they were regarded as having been polluted, but at other times it was suggested that they had been humanized, making eating them a form of cannibalism.

The assumption that animals could be agents in sexual encounters was expressed in other ways as well. They might even be hauled into court so that judges would see whether the offensive act had taken place through observing their behaviour.[41] For example, Mary Hicks was a married woman living in the working-class area of Cripplegate in London. In 1677 she was brought before London's Central Criminal Court and accused of having sex with a dog. Unfortunately for her, when the dog was 'set on the Bar before the prisoner', he proved the allegation by 'wagging his tail, and making motions as it were to kiss her, which 'twas sworn she did do when she made that horrid use of him'.[42] Both parties were found guilty and Hicks was forced to watch her dog being hanged before she was executed. In Hicks's case the dog was judged to be partly accountable for what had taken place. Other animals, however, were proclaimed innocent of the foul deed. In another trial, this time involving a man and a donkey, the neighbours signed statements attesting to the donkey's 'virtuous' behaviour and the fact that she had 'never given occasion for scandal'. Unlike the man, the donkey was believed to have been a victim of bestial lusts rather than a participant: she was acquitted.[43] Such views were a world away from current understandings, in which animals are stripped of all agency, and are therefore regarded as victims rather than co-conspirators. I will be challenging the relevance of this assumption in the final chapter of this book.

Human Harms

If the first and second important considerations in understanding legal responses to bestiality are theological and historical, the third has been driven by concerns for human well-being combined with paternalistic impulses to protect humans from their own sexual acts. This was what we saw in relation to the uproar over Pinyan's death. Mistaking an animal's consent to sexual intercourse can be dangerous. Dogs have teeth; horses and cows, powerful thighs. This was probably what killed a sixty-year-old farmer in Rome in 2009. According to neighbours, he was 'very close to his animals, in particular to the calf. In fact, he often spoke to it and treated it as a friend.'[44] When he was found, he was semi-naked and had been crushed to death.

Given that the most common choice of animal partner is a dog, the physiological reasons for injury (particularly if the act is interrupted before the dog ejaculated) interests physicians.[45] Close analysis of the anatomy of the male canine's penis reveals that, after a dog's penis is inserted into a vulva or anus, the pars longa glandis can double in diameter and its thickness can increase by up to 3 centimetres (1¼ in.). The bulbis glandis triples in width (that is, by 6 centimetres/2¼ in. or more) and can swell by up to 4 centimetres (1½ in.) in thickness. Peak pressures within this gland can reach 1,280 mmHg.[46] Once the two glands have been distended, they are effectively locked or 'tied', allowing the other distal penile structures to telescope back and forth over the penile bone. This movement can continue for between 5 and 45 minutes.[47] A very large volume of semen (up to 30 cc) is released.[48] Disproportionate size or excessive vigour can cause injury to the tissues of the rectum or colon of the human participant. Serious injuries occur if a human participant attempts to disengage with the dog before detumescence. At the very least, the injuries are similar to those inflicted through severe anal fisting.[49]

There are other dangers. Zoonosis (that is, infections that can be transmitted from animals to humans) is a risk, albeit a low one, especially when compared to all the other dangers associated with human–animal interactions such as meat-eating. Bestial sex could result in some very serious diseases, such as penile cancer.[50] Some medical research showed a correlation between sexual intercourse with animals and Parkinson's disease. The causal link is unclear, however: did bestiality cause Parkinson's or did the pharmacologic treatment for Parkinson's lead to 'adverse behavioral manifestations', such as zoophilia?[51]

Despite these disease implications, there is relatively little medical research into the risks of bestiality. In one survey of medical journals between 1948 and 2014, the author found fewer than twenty scientific papers investigating the potential medical effects of human–animal sexual interactions.[52]

It is also worth asking whether potential medical risks should justify state regulation of human behaviour. A lot of human practices are innately dangerous (including skiing, mountain climbing and having unprotected sex), but this is not used as an argument for criminalizing them. More to the point, many non-sexual practices that involve animals are known to be hazardous: eating chicken is just one example. Concerns about the spread of zoonoses should focus on dead animals (where the risk is immeasurably higher) rather than living ones.[53] Furthermore, not only is sex with animals a very inefficient means of transmitting disease,[54] but most cases of bestiality involve animals who are already domesticated.

Culture Wars

The religious, historical and paternalistic explanations for legal constructions of bestiality are important to understanding what happened in relation to human–animal sexual activities after the Second World War, when the seriousness of the offence was progressively reduced. In Britain, the u.s. and much of Europe bestiality was increasingly removed from the list of felonies, appearing instead under legislation dealing with cruelty to animals, breach of the peace, trespass, damage to property or offences to public decency. The medicalization of bestiality also brought with it some sympathy for certain offenders, although not, as we shall see, those who were dubbed 'degenerates' or violent criminals. As a consequence, in 1984, when Colin Higson appealed against his two-year prison sentence for attempting to bugger his Pyrenean Mountain bitch, the court decided to reduce the sentence to a probation order. This was done partly on the grounds that 'When all is said and done, it is the appellant and indeed his wife, and not the dog, who need help,' as the court report put it.[55]

However, in 2000 the UK Home Office reiterated its belief that bestiality should be considered an offence against sexual morals, as opposed to only an issue of animal welfare. In *Setting the Boundaries: Reforming the Law of Sex Offences* the Home Office contended that sex with animals should remain a criminal offence because bestiality 'offended against the dignity of animals and of people'. Animals were unable to consent to sexual activity with humans, they asserted, which was why legal systems had to remain in place in order to 'protect animals' from this 'profoundly disturbed behaviour'.[56] This approach represented a broader concern with concepts such as dignity, consent and rights.

The legal situation was less clear-cut in post-war America. As in Britain, the trend was moving away from prosecuting bestiality through legislation relating to crimes against 'nature' or morality and towards an emphasis on harm or cruelty. Also similar to Britain, the decriminalization of male homosexuality from the 1960s had a major effect on legal attitudes to bestiality. The introduction by the American Law Institute of the Model Penal Code (1962) was particularly important because, in the interests of modernizing state penal codes, it removed 'crimes against nature' and 'sodomy' from the statute books. This inadvertently decriminalized sex with animals. Liberal attitudes were furthered even more in 2003 with the Supreme Court's decision in *Lawrence* v. *Texas*, which led to the conclusion that sodomy statutes violated the Constitution's guarantee of due process.[57] Sexual activity that took place in private became more difficult to regulate.

Even sex education books for children mirrored these more liberal approaches. Take, for example, Jane Cousins's *Make It Happy*, a sex-education book written for thirteen- to sixteen-year-olds. This was an influential book, selling more than 10,000 copies and winning the *Times Educational Supplement*'s senior information book award. In the 1978 and 1986 editions, Cousins observed that 'some people feel sexually attracted to animals.' She informed her young readers,

It's not against the law to kiss, masturbate or be masturbated by an animal. But it is illegal for a woman or a man to have inter-course or buggery with an animal. It is totally impossible for a

woman to get pregnant by having sex with an animal – or for
an animal to get pregnant by having sex with a man.[58]

The backlash to such liberal approaches was swift. George Gardiner,
Conservative Party MP for Reigate, scolded Cousins for treating
'bestiality and incest in a totally neutral and amoral way'.[59] By its
1988 edition the paragraph on bestiality in *Make It Happy* had been
cut and, reflecting the AIDS epidemic, the book's main title had
been changed to *Make It Happy, Make It Safe*.[60]

People who enjoyed sexual relations with non-human animals
justifiably feared this criminalization of their activities. They
contended that anti-bestiality laws represent a 'witch hunt'.[61]
They even worried that the upsurge of sociological interest
in their communities would be damaging. At the very least,
the interest drew public attention to their proclivities.[62]

They were right to be concerned. Anti-liberal voices could
be heard complaining that the relaxation of laws against
homosexuality were opening the door to the legitimation of
bestiality. In 2003, for example, U.S. Senator Rick Santorum
complained that 'if the Supreme Court says that you have the
right to consensual [gay] sex within your home, then you have
the right to bigamy, you have the right to polygamy, you have the
right to incest, you have the right to adultery.' Gay sex, Santorum
contended, was similar to 'man on child, man on dog, or whatever
the case may be . . . And that's sort of where we are in today's world,
unfortunately. The idea is that the state doesn't have rights to limit
individuals' wants and passions.'[63] The philosopher Ralph McInerny
also argued that liberalizing laws to allow same-sex marriage
'heartens those who want to push on to overcoming superstitions
about bestiality'. He maintained that

> Their case is crystal clear. Marriage is the provision of mutual
> venereal pleasure. Both animals and humans are capable of

venereal pleasure and capable of providing it to one another. For them to do so constitutes marriage in any defensible sense of the term. There is, then, no intellectual obstacle to the union of man and beast.[64]

Organizations such as the Animal Sexual Abuse Information and Resource Site (ASAIRS) were established, devoted to rooting out all sightings of bestialists. ASAIRS was founded by Mike Rollands, a former zoo from Missouri. Rolland pointed out that its goal was to 'outlaw bestiality, specifically in the language of the law . . . Most important is adding the psychiatric intervention to get people to stop this. I believe that coming out, boasting about [having sex with] animals, is a cry for help. Because normal people don't do this.'[65] A similiar point was made as recently as 2017 by Mark Kumpf, director of the Montgomery County Animal Resource Center, speaking about a law banning bestiality in Ohio: 'It's a crime that defies explanation to the rational person,' he maintained, adding, 'We're dealing with a different species' – by which he was not talking about the animal partner. Bestialists were not human.[66]

Rollands went even further. He revealed the names of University of Indiana sociologists who wrote to the Missouri House of Representatives arguing against the adoption of HB 1658, a clause that would prohibit bestiality. It was, Rollands insisted, 'war time' because

If you allow two zoophile friendly doctors who probably never met a zoophile in person nor saw their animals to stop legislation in a state they don't even live in, then you can expect they will try to remove the laws in ALL the rest of the states using that as an example.[67]

Rolland successfully mobilized religious and social conservatives to pass the law. ASAIRS also argued that states should mandate psychological counselling for everyone who was convicted of bestial offences.[68] Despite this, Roland worried that counsellors might not be concerned for the welfare of the animal. He observed that therapists were 'not animal welfare activists, but human activists . . . The therapist is trained and hired to work for their human patient's happiness as long as they're not harming other people. They have no way of knowing whether the animal is being harmed or not.'[69] ASAIRS and the First Strike campaign (a project run by the Humane Society of the United States and aimed at reporting cases of abuse and educating people to recognize sexual cruelty against animals) were powerful lobbyists in the criminalization of bestiality.

This was the context within which legal frameworks concerning human–animal relations were revised. While very few states designated bestiality a felony in 1990, by the start of the twenty-first century, 24 states had made it so. By 2017 this had risen to 42 states.[70] There was no consistency in what exactly was proscribed. In some states the animal had to be injured; others required genital penetration while ignoring oral sex. Unlike the legislation that had been passed in the 1990s, state legislatures in the twenty-first century re-emphasized the view that bestiality was an offence against morals. This was due to anxieties concerning acts that did not lead to obvious physical harm to the animals, such as the numerous abuses that had been filmed taking place on Pinyan's farm, as well as Internet advertisements that promoted the use of animals for sexual purposes.[71] A sense of moral outrage permeated this new wave of legislation. In Rhode Island, for example, the law against bestiality described it as 'the abominable and detestable crime against nature'. In contrast, Rhode Island's statute against sexual assault of a child lacked the graphic moral outrage, merely stating that 'First degree child molestation sexual assault occurs when there is sexual intercourse . . . between a minor who is 14 or younger, and a defendant of any age.'[72] This new, censorious attitude forged a unique alliance between animal rights activists and religious fundamentalists.[73]

Criminalization

But what exactly was being criminalized? As we saw in the debates surrounding the criminalization of bestiality in the State of Washington, part of the problem was that politicians and jurists were reluctant to talk about 'disgusting' behaviour. In many jurisdictions descriptions of what actually constituted a 'crime against nature' were entirely absent. 'Crimes against nature', decreed one court official, involved 'the disgrace of human nature by an unnatural sexual gratification of which reason and delicacy forbids a more detailed description'.[74] In the *State* v. *Bonynge* case (1990) in Minnesota, it was pointed out that the term 'carnal knowledge' had human connotations: how could it sensibly be used to refer to sexual intercourse between humans and animals?[75] It was even unclear whether bestiality was actually the same thing as 'sodomy': what if the intercourse were not *per anum*?[76] And were all animals 'beasts' in law? In *Murray* v. *State of Indiana* (1957), for example, the defendant appealed against his conviction for having sexual connection with a chicken (in which the chicken died) by arguing that the clause specified that the 'abominable and detestable crime against nature' had to involve a 'beast'. Was a fowl a 'beast'? Or was a 'beast' 'any four-footed animal', as some dictionaries stipulated?[77] In 2006 Jeffrey Haynes successfully appealed against being placed on Michigan's public sex offender register on the grounds that the sheep, Thelma, whom he 'sodomized' was not an 'individual' in law.[78]

Even the definition of 'sexual' was unclear. For example, the UK's Sexual Offences Act of 2003 declared that a bestial offence is committed if a man intentionally performs an act of penetration with his penis and what is penetrated is the vagina or anus of a living animal and he knows or is reckless as to whether that is what is penetrated. An offence is also committed where the perpetrator allows or causes her vagina or her anus to be penetrated by the penis of a living animal and the perpetrator is reckless as to whether that is what he or she is being penetrated by.[79]

It is a curious wording. After all, it only proscribes acts involving penetration with a penis (either an animal's or a man's). It neither covers penetration by a finger or fist, nor criminalizes cunnilingus or fellatio with an animal. There are a host of other 'sexual' acts about which it remains silent.

The chief problem, however, was the one mentioned in the Pinyan case: how could bestial acts be differentiated from routine procedures in animal husbandry? Indeed, these activists point out, sexual and non-sexual forms of harm are indistinguishable. Dairy cows are, in effect, sexual workers, being kept continuously pregnant. Dairy farmers use a 'rape rack' to forcibly restrain a cow while she is impregnated by a bull or artificially. Humans engage in 'foreplay' to arouse animals prior to insemination. Animals are spayed, neutered, castrated; they have their genitals restricted. Standard farming practices include the castration of pigs and the manual or electrical stimulation of the genitals of bulls to collect the semen. Male animals are often castrated in the interests of 'meat quality' and to make them 'easier to handle'.[80] Analgesics are often not available, and the side effects of some of these procedures include open wounds, pain, haemorrhage, eventration (the prolapse of a part of the small intestine into the inguinal canal), infection and tetanus.[81]

Clearly, though, anti-bestiality laws had to protect veterinarians and other people engaged in 'accepted animal husbandry practices that provide necessary care for animals bred for commercial purposes', in the words of jurists in Arizona.[82] The insemination of farm animals required particular exemptions. The artificial insemination of pigs, for example, sometimes requires farmers to simulate mounting and fondling. The insemination of cows is equally personal, as indicated by the *Farmers Weekly*. Its '8-step Guide to Artificially Inseminating a Dairy Cow' (2015) instructs farmers to begin by ensuring that the cow is 'relaxed' as well as 'appropriately restrained'. After the straw containing the semen has thawed and been placed in the 'AI gun', farmers are required to 'prepare the cow's vulva with a paper towel and put on a full-arm glove and lubricant'. They are told to

> Insert your arm into the cow, by forming a cone with your fingers while keeping the tail aside with your other hand . . . The initial landmark is the cervix and this should be located before inserting the gun . . . After locating the cervix, use the elbow to exert downward pressure on the vagina. This will part the lips of the vulva for the AI gun. The lips should be wiped clean, with the gun inserted past the vestibule and into the vagina . . . The semen should be deposited into the short chamber of the uterine horns . . . Deposit the semen slowly, by counting 5, 4, 3, 2, 1.[83]

Artificial insemination of a dairy cow.

Anti-bestial legislation had to differentiate such penetrative practices from ones motivated by sexual desire. In other words, the problem was not so much about the small number of people who engage in sexual intercourse with farm animals but about how certain intimate acts involving the sexual organs of animals stood in relation to capitalist systems of production and reproduction. This focus was even more evident in American states where, in seeking to protect the farming industry, 'ag-gag' laws were introduced, criminalizing animal rights activists who reported animal abuse on farms or in factories.[84] By reporting painful insemination practices, these activists directly threatened farm profits. In other words, the difference between a bestialist and a farmer was a biopolitical one. The bestialist manipulated the sex organs of animals in the interest of personal gratification; in contrast, farmers similarly manipulated the animal's sexual organs but in the interest of capitalist production. The first act was criminalized; the second, promoted as necessary to economic growth.

Animal liberationist Karen Davis, the president of United Poultry Concerns, was incensed by such practices, maintaining that animal farming is 'sexually abusive in essence'. Controlling the sexual lives of animals is central to farming practices: indeed, it is impossible to distinguish between the 'production' of meat and the manipulation of animal sex organs. Davis insists that animal-farming 'invites lascivious conduct' towards '"food" animals on the part of producers and consumers alike'.[85] She points out that 'humans engage in oral intercourse with unconsenting [sic] non-human animals every time they put a piece of an animal's body inside their mouth.' Omnivorous humans over the age of fifty are 'walking around with half their internal organs having been taken by force from creatures they think it demeaning of our species to have sex with'.[86] Davis's view is extreme but consistent: people who oppose bestiality must resist every form of animal exploitation. These are the debates we turn to next.

Two

Cruelty to Animals

Define: **Trigger Warning.**
A statement alerting people to the fact that what
follows contains potentially distressing material.

Some chapters should come with a health warning. This is one
of them.

You know what to expect: the title of this chapter clearly
states that we will be addressing deliberate acts of cruelty. Actually,
it is going to be much worse than that. We are going to look at a
particularly harrowing form of violence: rape.

Given humans' long history of exploiting animals, the fact that
we sexually abuse them as well is hardly surprising. Sexual assault
is one of many ways we harm animals. Readers who are neither
vegetarian nor vegan may want to think about why discussing
the sexual abuse of animals is so upsetting, especially when we
consider all the other terrible things many people do to them.
Animals are slaughtered; their skin is fashioned into handbags;
their flesh is cooked and eaten. Violence is intrinsic to human–
animal interactions. Yet the *sexual* part of 'sexual violence' is
nevertheless particularly revolting to people, even to carnivorous
leather fetishists.

Sexual violence is highly gendered. In this chapter I take seriously
the feminist insight that draws a relationship between the sexual
abuse of non-human animals and that of human girls and women.
An extreme version of this argument has been made by feminist
scholar Catharine A. MacKinnon. In her essay entitled 'Of Mice and
Men: A Feminist Fragment on Animal Rights' (2004), MacKinnon

claims: 'Most states have provisions against bestiality, which in substance are laws against doing sexually to animals what is done to women by men on a daily basis. These laws define it as immoral for men to treat animals as they treat women free of legal restraints.'[1] She is overstating her case: after all, not only are there laws prohibiting non-consensual sexual intercourse with human women, but it is also a fact that laws prohibiting bestiality are an ineffective form of restraint. However, her comment about the law's relative lack of interest in '*meaningful* consent' to sex by women and non-human animals is well made. This is why I start this chapter with the coterminous sexual abuse of a female human called Linda and a male dog called Norman.

Linda Lovelace

Linda Susan Boreman (aka Linda Lovelace) was raised in Yonkers, New York. As a child, she fantasized about becoming a nun. By 1970, when she was 21, her ambition had changed to marrying a loving man and raising children. Two years later, her sadistic partner and pimp Chuck Traynor, along with film producer Robert Wolf, forced her at gunpoint to make a pornographic film that involved having sex with a short-haired, tan-coloured dog named Norman. Unlike Lovelace – about whom we know a great deal – little is known about Norman, except that he could 'go' (that is, have sex) 'all night and all day' and was 'beady-eyed'.[2] When he looked at Lovelace, she 'had the eerie sensation that he knew more about what was going to happen than I did'.[3] The silent 8mm stag film was released under a number of titles, including *Dog 1*, *Dog Fucker*, *Dog-a-Rama* and *Dogarama*. As with 99 per cent of films in this genre, it depicted a woman (rather than a man) engaging in sexual acts with a non-human animal.[4]

Although *Dogarama* became notorious within a pornographic subculture, its popularity never reached the heights of *Deep Throat*,

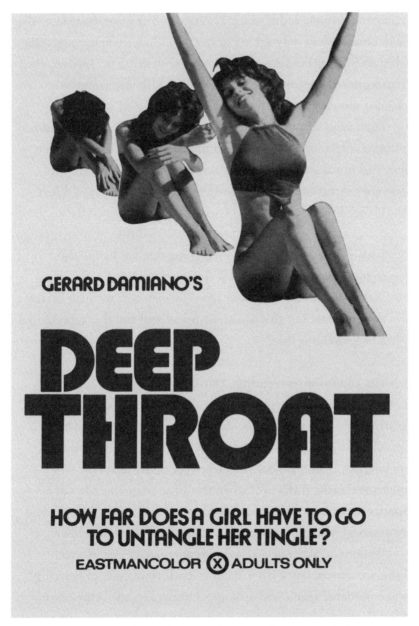

Poster for *Deep Throat* (1972, dir. Gerard Damiano), starring Linda Lovelace (born Linda Susan Boreman).

a human-on-human film which Lovelace and Traynor made later that year. Lovelace had only agreed to star in both of these pornographic films after being beaten and threatened with death by Traynor. *Deep Throat* grossed approximately $100 million, although some estimates claim it was closer to $600 million.

Eight years after the release of *Dogarama*, Lovelace published her account of filming it. She revealed that if she could have 'foreseen how bad it was going to be', she 'wouldn't have surrendered' to Traynor's threats and 'would have chosen the possibility of death'. She claimed that

> I am able to handle almost everything that has happened
> to me in my life . . . but I'm still not able to handle that day.
> A dog. An animal. I've been raped by men who were no better
> than animals, but this was an actual animal and that represented
> a huge dividing line.[5]

Her confession is revealing. During her years with Traynor, Lovelace suffered multiple insults and assaults, including rape, beatings and anal sadism, but she regarded being forced to have sex with a dog as a fate worse than death. The suffering inflicted on Lovelace by the 'bestial' men who repeatedly raped her was multiplied many times over when the 'beast' was a member of a species for whom consent was also deemed irrelevant. No one asked Norman whether he consented; no one asked Lovelace, either.

Within the hyper-sexualized pornographic circles in which Lovelace moved, fantasizing about or performing acts of bestiality was considered risqué and arousing. Lovelace recalled that playboy Hugh Hefner would spend hours 'rapping about sex with animals'. He admitted that he had tried several times to 'get a girl and a dog together'.[6] In addition, *Dogarama* was not the first time Traynor had attempted to get Lovelace to commit bestiality. Before that film, Traynor had intended to drive Lovelace to Juárez (Mexico) to watch her and other women having sex with a donkey. The 'event' was planned to take place in a sporting pit surrounded by customers who would lay bets on how many centimetres of the donkey's penis each woman could accommodate in her vagina. Traynor told Lovelace what to expect:

> The chicks [women] go in one at a time . . . And the crowd cheers, just like when prizefighters come into a ring. And then they strap the chick up on this contraption and then they bring out their trained donkey and they lead the donkey right into the fucking cunt . . . They've got to point him right, you dig? Sometimes the chick gets ripped up a little – I'm telling you, you haven't lived 'till you've seen one of those donkey dongers. Those suckers are *huge*.[7]

Fortunately for Lovelace, a car accident prevented them arriving in Juárez, so Traynor purchased a dog named Rufus with the intentions of coercing Lovelace to have sexual intercourse with him instead. On this occasion, however, Lovelace had taken advice from a performer who specialized in 'making love to dogs'. Lovelace was advised to

> wait for the animal to come to you. Stay in just one spot and let him take all the time in the world. If you move at all, he may get scared off. A dog doesn't like it when you back away or make any moves toward it . . . And whatever else you do, don't touch it [the dog's penis] directly. You'll scare the dog to death.

Lovelace took the advice to heart, but simply reversed the guidelines. When she acted in a way that dogs found sexually aggressive, Rufus 'backed off' and refused to perform.[8] In this way, both Lovelace and Rufus were able to exert some agency, albeit within limits set by an abusive husband and a predatory owner.

Although Lovelace approached acts of sexual intercourse between humans and animals with loathing, she admitted that her entire world at that time was 'bestial'. The millions of 'ordinary' men and women who flocked to see the film *Deep Throat*, in which Lovelace was literally raped on screen, participated in this theatre of degradation. Like other women in her milieu, Lovelace was referred to as an animal: she was just another 'chick'. The pornographers were a 'Wolf' and animal 'trainer/Traynor'. When describing the multiple rapes, Lovelace routinely characterized her assailants as 'animals' who treated her 'as though I was a piece of meat'.[9]

Linda Lovelace and Chuck Traynor, c. 1972.

Unsurprisingly, she was deeply scarred by her sex acts with human as well as non-human animals. But it was the forced act of bestiality with Norman that was most painful. She recalled:

> There were no greater humiliations left for me. The memory of that day and that dog does not fade the way other memories do. The overwhelming sadness that I felt on that day is with me at this moment, stronger than ever. It was a bad day, such a bad day.[10]

Battered Pets

Ironically, it was the success of *Deep Throat* that eventually enabled Lovelace to escape from Traynor's grip. No escape was possible for Norman, Rufus or the unnamed donkey, however: they were nothing more than commodities to be exploited.

Such lack of attention to the pain and suffering of animals is commonplace – and not only among pornographers and rapists. Even philosophers, scientists, pet owners and zoophiles might act as though animals are not capable of 'truly' feeling pain. Most famously, René Descartes insisted that animals were mere automata or moving machines, driven by instinct alone. For Descartes, animals' screams of pain were simply mechanical responses that functioned as a form of human moral edification.[11] Later commentators speculated that, at the very least, there might be a 'Great Chain of Feeling' in which some sentient creatures (European males, for example) were more attuned to physical sensation than other sentient creatures (such as women, slaves and non-human animals).[12] As late as 1991, Peter Harrison published an article in the influential journal *Philosophy* entitled 'Do Animals Feel Pain?' in which he argued against the full sentience of non-human animals. He contended that only creatures who can '*think*' can have consciousness of pain; and animals (according to him) slip below the threshold of 'real' consciousness.[13]

Are people who love their pets more attuned to animals' feelings? Controlling the sexual proclivities of pets is routine: in the UK and U.S., over 80 per cent of dogs and 90 per cent of cats are spayed and neutered, for example. At the other extreme, many dogs (especially 'purebreds') are forced to reproduce. As one dog-breeder contended, 'Breeding was a profitable business, so bitches had to be bred from whether they liked it or not; if they weren't willing they were helped, if they wouldn't be helped they were forced, and many a time [I'd] seen them muzzled and put into a sling to prevent them resisting.'[14] Like women, pets might be particularly vulnerable to abuse within the privacy of their own homes. The physical abuse of pets often includes sexual elements. One veterinary survey of 448 'battered pets' found evidence of sexual assault in 6 per cent of the animals.[15]

In bestialist and zoophilic circles, too, animals are often treated as 'things'. It is impossible to know the extent of the abuse. Some studies, such as one based in Germany during the 1960s, concluded that an incredible 70 per cent of zoophilic acts were violent, even sadistic.[16] However, most surveys reveal *low* levels of sexual sadism among online zoo communities.[17] Andrea M. Beetz's study of 113 men who practised bestiality revealed that over 5 per cent confessed that they had harmed an animal at least once. Just under 10 per cent admitted to having at least once used force during sexual acts with animals.[18] Whatever the accuracy of such statistics, bestialists were generally unrepentant about causing injury, including bruising vaginas, battering cloacas, causing internal bleeding and even killing their animals.

Treating animals as sexual 'things' is also prominent in the meat industry. In the words of one meatpacker, 'There's lots of it, all the time y'know – Sex with sheep.' He explained that 'you can do it best with a sheep. You can pick them up by putting your hand up their rib cage, or up their arse, basically, 'cause there's a big hole where their tails bin [*sic*] cut off.'[19] PETA filmed and publicized numerous

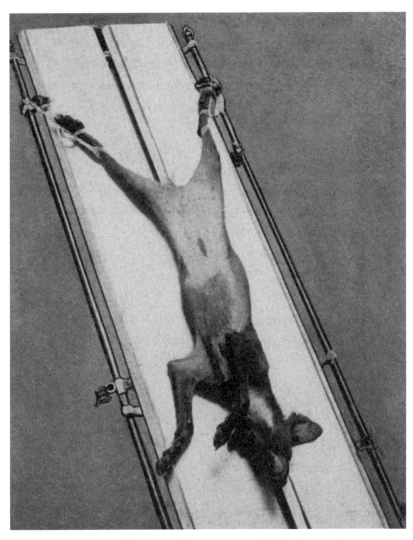

The practical mode of restraint for spaying, with the dog under anaesthesia, in George R. White, *Animal Castration* (1920).

incidents.[20] Animal protectionists seeking to expose such violence are themselves prosecuted under 'ag-gag' laws, which criminalize reporting abuse.[21]

There are many other ways sentient creatures can be harmed. As in debates about sex between humans, there are important distinctions to be made between an animal who engages in enthusiastic participation and those who exhibit non-consent (resistance), avoidance behaviours or passive acquiescence. Some animals are able to resist sexual activity by biting or scratching. This was why the Happy Horse-man Mark Matthews, a devoted zoophile, rejected the idea that his sexual exchanges with horses were abusive. He believed that 'the horses didn't seem to mind . . . It wasn't like it was rape or anything!' He scoffed at 'the idea of *raping* a horse . . . standing naked behind an animal with powerful legs and hard, sharp hooves, [my] genitals swinging free and vulnerable, trying to do something the animal didn't like'.[22]

Other animals (such as Lovelace's Rufus) simply avoided sexual encounters by failing to 'perform' the required action. In an essay entitled 'Sexual Relations with Animals (Zoophilia): An Unrecognized Problem in Animal Welfare Legislation' (2005), Swiss legal experts Gieri Bolliger and Antoine F. Goetschel acknowledged that 'zoophilic relationships can be mutual' and animals 'can develop strong affections for people', which may include a libidinal aspect. However, just because it isn't difficult for 'some animals to enter into an intimate relationship with a person' and be sexually aroused, 'in general, an animal only does this if it is used to such behaviour' or has been 'trained to perform such behaviour'. They argued that 'such conditioning does not only infringe upon the free sexual development of an animal' but risks creating 'strong dependency' of the animal on his or her human owner. For them, the 'violation of an animal's sexual integrity . . . does not depend upon the question of what an animal feels during a zoophilic act, but rather whether such an act complies with its free will'.[23]

Even in the absence of overt coercion, animals are vulnerable to being abused. Many are bred to be docile, so they are unable to resist a determined human; they are also 'groomed' and made dependent on the goodwill of their human owners.[24] Their agency is curtailed. This is why animal rights campaigners can often be heard maintaining that most animals resemble infants and children, are what philosopher Tom Regan called 'moral patients' (similar, for example, to people with intellectual disabilities), in their inability to give meaningful consent.[25] According to these arguments, people are required to honour the 'dignity' of other species, which means protecting them from 'humiliation, excessive exploitation, and interference'. This is similar to the way adults attempt to protect children.[26] We are back to MacKinnon's insistence on *meaningful consent to sex*.

Interspecies Sexual Assault

One of the most prominent advocates of the argument that *all* sex with animals is abusive is sociologist Piers Beirne. In a series of highly influential essays published in the 1990s and early 2000s, Beirne argued that bestiality 'almost always involve[s] coercion'. Because 'we will never know if animals are able to assent – in their terms – to human suggestions for sexual intimacy,' bestiality should be renamed 'interspecies sexual assault'.[27] Like infants, young children and other 'moral patients', animals are 'without an effective voice'.[28] Importantly, they cannot communicate their abuse to third parties.[29] Beirne admitted that, by introducing the term 'interspecies sexual assault', critics might accuse him of diluting the horror of sexual assault of (human) women. However, Bierne contends that this is an unwarranted anxiety. Following the claims of Carol Adams, which she made in *The Sexual Politics of Meat: A Feminist-Vegetarian Critical Theory* (1990), Beirne argued that 'Sexism and speciesism operate not in opposition to each other but in tandem. Interspecies sexual assault is the product of a masculinity that sees women, animals, and nature as objects that can be controlled, manipulated, and exploited.'[30] It was a comment that resonated with Lovelace's experiences during the making of *Dogarama* and *Deep Throat*.

This comparison between the abuse of animals and of women has merit. As I argue in *What It Means to Be Human* (2011), women have historically been designated as closer to non-human animal life in the 'Great Chain of Being'.[31] Misogynist humour routinely classifies women as animals (pussies, chicks, birds, vixens, cows and bitches, for instance) and many of the arguments about whether women should have the vote were countered by opponents who insisted that women were, like non-human animals, not sufficiently rational to be granted such a responsibility. Women's status as not fully human has excused a multiple of cruelties, including harms involving sexual relations.

The close connection between the sexual abuse of women and that of animals has led veterinary physicians to extrapolate from procedures associated with collecting evidence in cases of the rape of human females to that of non-human animals. In *Veterinary Forensics* (2007), for example, Melinda Merck provides vets with lengthy instructions based on human sexual assault protocols on how to carry out physical examinations on animals suspected of having been sexually harmed. She also gives advice on 'best practice' in taking evidence from the scene of the alleged crime as well as from the suspected perpetrator.[32] Similarly, in 2008 Ranald Munro, Professor of Forensic Veterinary Pathology at the Royal Veterinary College, London, and Helen Munro, a fellow at the University of Edinburgh Veterinary School, recommended using rape kits designed for humans to test for the abuse of animals.[33] It is a move also championed by Martha Smith-Blackmore of the Animal Rescue League of Boston, although for slightly different reasons. For Smith-Blackmore the advantage of using the official rape kit devised for humans is that it displays the state's logo prominently on the box. This sends 'a message to the court that this is a sexual assault case', she insists, adding that it reveals through the 'way it's packaged and presented' that the sexual abuse of animals is 'the same as assaults against people'.[34]

While some of the psychiatrists discussed in the last chapter argued that animal abusers and child abusers were one and the same people, animal activists argued by analogy. For them, 'interspecies sexual assault' was analogous to child sexual abuse. Indeed, Beirne explicitly borrowed his concept from discourses surrounding paedophilia.[35] Both forms of abuse, animal activists argued, had been silenced. Child sexual abuse had only entered into public discourse in the 1980s; now it was time for animal sexual abuse to similarly become noticed.[36] In the U.S. many animal welfare groups and activists were inspired by compulsory state and national registers for sex offenders. They proposed establishing Animal Abuse Registries similar to those that paedophiles were required to sign. This would help law enforcement authorities, as well as activists, police the movements of offenders.[37] The 2001 model law written by the Animal Legal Defence Fund and called the Offender Registration and Community Notification law for animal abuse also notifies people who sell pets or place animals up for adoption of animal abusers in their midst. The problems with such registers, not surprisingly, mirror their counterparts in the child abuse field: they do not prevent recidivism, they isolate offenders and drive them underground, they fail to protect animals, they are a form of public shaming, they invade personal privacy and they are costly. The failure of many jurisdictions to adopt this proposal has led to the establishment of independent databases, the most important ones being Through Their Eyes (TTA) and the Animal Abuse Registry Database Administrative System (AARDA at Pet-Abuse. com). However, these too are problematic: they are inaccurate and incomplete; the volunteer staff, unaccountable.

Pornography

So far in this chapter, we have explored the sexual abuse of animals by pet owners, bestialists and zoophiles. However, as we saw in the case of Lovelace, Norman, Rufus and the unnamed donkey, the sexual abuse of animals in pornography is big business. The Internet is saturated with depictions of bestiality, including dedicated porn sites. In the past, much of this porn was filmed and produced in the Netherlands and Denmark, with other major producers residing in the U.S., Brazil, Japan and Sweden. Today, with the democratization of technologies of producing and distributing photographic as well as filmic images (as in social media, for example), anyone with the inclination and some fairly basic technologies can upload bestiality porn onto the Internet.

Unsurprisingly, then, bestiality porn is extremely varied. Animals are bought and sold in bestiality forums.[38] There are commercial organizations devoted to selling zoophilic toys, including silicone penises in the shape of the sex organs of dogs, hyenas, cats, horses and kangaroos. For example, among many other sex toys, www.zoofur.com features a dildo named RuffStuff, which measures 2.5 centimetres (1 in.) across the tip, 19.7 centimetres (7¾ in.) from tip to base and 5.7 centimetres (2 in.) across the knot. The knot itself is about 3.8 centimetres (1½ in.) tall. Visitors to the site are told that RuffStuff is 'great for beginners', because 'Ruff has seen plenty of action and is certainly more than willing to show off his skills.' Ruff promises to 'make any ordinary night into something extraordinary . . . and Ruff is more than willing to go home with you'.

Although sex toys are profitable, it is nevertheless the case that the depiction of real humans engaging in sex with actual animals dominates Internet sites. Nearly all the human participants are female. In one major survey of over a hundred websites involving bestiality or zoophilia, only one featured a human male engaged in a sex act (he was being fellated by a goat); in this exception, though, the man was standing next to a naked woman.[39] The animals are typically either male or genderless.[40] Even viewers who find cross-species genital interactions visually attractive cannot help noticing that the women are routinely depicted in positions that are intended to be humiliating; more often than not, the animal looks confused.[41]

Bodil Joensen.

As well as being misogynous, there are also markedly racist elements to these portrayals: a high proportion show Black women engaging in sex with animals or even dressed up as animals themselves.

Nevertheless, the most famous of the zoo-porn actresses was the blonde bombshell Danish actress Bodil Joensen. Unlike Lovelace, Joensen enjoyed her sexual encounters with animals, particularly with her collie, called Lassie. Between the late 1960s and the early 1970s, Joensen made around forty zoo films.[42] She was also extremely popular in live sex shows that she would perform in clubs. According to one account, 'As soon as the ever ready and horny Collie heard their theme music strike up (the naughty pop song "Je t'aime") and saw the stage light go on, he would storm the stage in eager anticipation.' Joensen would appear – either naked or in 'a soon-to-be-discarded bra and panties'.[43] And the sex show would begin. It is impossible to know to what extent Lassie was groomed to participate in this pornographic theatre. Joensen was also active in sex tourism, often hiring out her farm and its residents for pornographic auditions.[44] She well deserves the title 'Queen of Bestiality'.

The films made by Joensen and her many animal lovers were sexually graphic, but they were not violent. At the other extreme are pornographers specializing in 'crush videos'. These videos are highly sexual, usually featuring a woman clad in high heels (typically bright red stilettos) crushing live animals to death with her feet. Nancy Perry, Vice President for Government Affairs in the Humane Society of the United States, observed that the videos consisted of

> Scantily clad, high-heeled women stomping, squishing, and impaling animals to death. The animals are often secured so they cannot escape, but are free enough to move so that their writhing in agony is clear to the viewer. This sickening torment is drawn out for many minutes intentionally, and even for hours, during which time the animal's cries, moans, and squeals are actually highlighted along with their excretions of blood, urine, intestines, and even organs as they are crushed to death.[45]

The animals involved are primarily rabbits, puppies and kittens, but films can be viewed in which monkeys, pigs and goats are crushed. Such videos had been marketed to sexual fetishists since the 1950s, and proliferated with the Internet. Prior to 1999, when the U.S. Congress passed the Depiction of Animal Cruelty Act, there were over 2,000 crush videos in circulation, each of which could be sold over the Internet for as much as $300. Annual sales were estimated at nearly $1 million.[46] Crush videos were originally banned by Congress in 1999 but the debate was reignited in 2010 when the

U.S. Supreme Court struck down the ban on First Amendment grounds. In response, the Animal Crush Video Prohibition Act of 2010 was passed, clarifying that 'certain extreme acts of animal cruelty that appeal to a specific sexual fetish' constituted 'obscenity' and were therefore exempt from the protection of the First Amendment. However, some commentators questioned what was 'sexual' (and therefore 'obscene') about such videos, especially since they usually showed women only from their knees down and rarely revealed the sex organs of the animal victims. However, fetishists found them sexually gratifying, especially since the women carrying out the 'crush' typically talked to the animals 'in a dominatrix pattern or other sexual tones' in order to appeal to both sadistic and masochist viewers.[47]

Racism

So far, I have linked the sexual abuse of animals with violence against women. An important element has been left out, however: racism. Sexual encounters between different species have invariably focused on 'primitive' societies, miscegenation and human–animal hybrids. Since ancient times it was feared that sex across the species would lead to the birth of monsters. As Roman rhetorician Claudius Aelianus (commonly Aelian) warned in *On the Characteristics of Animals*: 'Many creatures are begotten with two faces and two breasts: some born of a cow have the foreparts of a man; others on the contrary spring up begotten of a man but with the head of a cow.'[48] When seventeenth-century diarist Samuel Pepys first encountered a 'great baboon', he concluded that it was 'so much like a man in most things, that (although they say there is a species of them) yet I cannot believe but that it is a monster got of a woman and a she-baboon'.[49] Popular folklore propagated such stories. One tale, recorded in the National Folklore Collection of Ireland, involved a woman who slept with her dog and subsequently gave birth to a child who 'had a dog's head on it'. The folklorists reported that the villagers 'would smother them sort of freaks'.[50] Indeed, the pseudo-scientific idea known as 'maternal impressions' did not even require the woman to have sexual intercourse with a 'beast' in order to create a monster: sincere affection was enough. Thus the American phrenologist Orson Squire Fowler, in *Creative and Sexual Science; or, Manhood, Womanhood, and Their Mutual Relations* (1904), described a pregnant woman who visited a menagerie and 'became deeply interested in its animals'. Five months later, she 'gave birth to a monster, some parts of which resembled one wild beast, and other parts other animals'.[51] Stories of interspecies hybrids continue throughout the modern period, and include the 'hybrids' in Erle C. Kenton's film *Island of Lost Souls* (1932), who were deliberately created in order to form a class of slaves.

Zoophiles themselves were often anxious that their sexual activities would bring forth a 'monster'. An unnamed zoophile who sent letters about his experiences to the sexologist R.E.L. Masters was clearly fixated by the 'possibility of interspecies monstrous issue', in part because it would have exposed his sexual preferences.[52] Indeed, as an adolescent, one of the female pigs he had sex with *did* give birth to a 'monstrous freak', and he was relieved when his father simply 'dismissed the occurrence as merely something unusual'.[53] This young zoophile was so convinced, though, that it was his offspring that he 'buried it under a tree, rather than allow it to be disposed of in the usual manner'.[54]

In slave-owning societies as well as during imperial forays, such fears took a viciously racist tone. Slave owners and colonial administrators routinely used interspecies sexual intercourse to bolster their sadistic bigotry. In Edward Long's offensive *History of Jamaica; or, General Survey of the Antient [sic] and Modern State* (1774), for example, he contended that orang-utans 'sometimes endeavor to surprise and carry off Negroe women into their woody retreats, in order to enjoy them'. He argued that apes 'conceive a passion for the Negroe women, and hence must be supposed to covet their embraces from a natural impulse of desire, such as inclines one animal towards another of the same species, or which has a conformity in the organs of generation'. In other words, he believed that 'the oran-outang and some races of black men are very nearly allied.'[55] This theory of polygenism – in which biologically different human species evolved separately – was part of the discreditable belief that Africans were of a different species to Europeans.

Commentators did not have to adhere to the idea of polygenism to repeat lurid tales in which 'tribal' women were at risk of being sexually molested by monkeys. In 1818, for example, the Scottish zoologist and physician Thomas Stewart Traill presented a paper to the Wernerian Natural History Society entitled 'Observations on the Anatomy of the Orang Outang'. He informed his distinguished audience that 'Negro girls' were often 'carried off' by Great Apes, with only a few managing to 'escape . . . to human society, after having been for years detained by their ravishers in a frightful captivity'.[56] The lascivious passion of apes for 'native' women was presented as a natural event in 'primitive' societies. Most famous is French sculptor Emmanuel Frémiet's *Gorilla Carrying Off a Woman* (1887), in which a male gorilla carries off a white woman. This life-sized sculpture is violent but was intended to be read also as erotic. The fact that the woman wears a gorilla's jawbone in her hair suggests that she, too, is part of a pillaging culture. Its appeal to fin de siècle audiences was immense. The sculpture was awarded a Medal of Honour from the Salon in Paris and a gold medal at the International Fine Arts Exhibition in Munich the following year. It has been reproduced in miniature millions of times.

An in-depth analysis of such views can be seen in a relentlessly offensive book called *Human Gorillas*, published in 1901 by Count Roscaud (almost certainly a pseudonym). *Human Gorillas* has a foreword by Sir Richard F. Burton, the famous explorer and diplomat, as well as editor of the unexpurgated English translation

Emmanuel Frémiet, *Gorilla Carrying Off a Woman*, 1887, bronze sculpture.

of *The Book of the Thousand Nights and a Night* (commonly called *The Arabian Nights*) and the *Kama Sutra*. Burton maintained that the fact that no one had ever presented proof of a 'mule' resulting from sexual intercourse between a human and an ape was sufficient to 'invalidate Darwinism'. He admitted that if such a human–ape hybrid had been born, it would most likely have been 'destroyed', but 'the fact of our never having found a trace of it except in legend and idle story seems to militate against its existence.'[57] However, Burton followed this statement with a comment that 'when . . . man shall become a "Homo sapiens"' (that is, a wise man), he would be able to 'cast off the prejudices of the cradle and the nursery and will ascertain by actual experiment if human being and monkey can breed together'. Although the resulting offspring would 'own half a soul', they might also 'prove most serviceable as a hewer of wood and a drawer of water, in fact as an agricultural labourer'.[58]

In the main text of *Human Gorillas*, Count Roscaud took Burton's reflections further. He also wondered whether sex between an ape and a human could result in offspring. Roscaud maintained that 'such unions are not prolific, for no African explorer has ever affirmed that he has met in any native village a creature half ape half man'.[59] Echoing Burton, he admitted that 'it would not be inconsistent with savage habits to put both the mother and the offspring – one can hardly say child – to death.'[60]

Roscaud's text then took a more novelistic turn. He took keen delight in relating a story by Émile Dodillon entitled *Hemo*. It was about an explorer and anthropologist called Jan Maas who built a hut on the edge of a forest in Guinea. One day he rescued a young female gorilla (who he named D'ginna) whose arm had become trapped in the cleft of a tree. After her arm had healed, he asked himself whether 'sexual connection' between a gorilla and a human would 'prove the natural identity', that is, the Darwinian link between the two species. If he succeeded in producing a child with a gorilla, Maas reasoned, would he not 'obtain that fame, that glory of science, the object of all his dreams, and for which he had suffered so much?'[61] With posterity in mind, he raped the young gorilla. In the author's words, Maas 'approached her, and believing that he was acting of his own free will and not actuated by the erithesmus [sic: meaning erethism, or state of abnormal sexual desire] of any vile desire, he seized D'ginna, who now resisted, and "married" her'.[62] The following morning, the 'enthusiasm of the experiment had passed away; his act appeared a diabolical temptation, and he considered himself as disgraced for ever.'[63] However, 'at night his memory was stronger than his remorse' and he resumed having sexual intercourse with

D'ginna. This continued until he observed that his 'mistress' was pregnant. He was 'horror-stricken', reflecting: 'I shall be dishonoured ... but immortal.' He realized that he might be driven 'out of all civilized countries' to ensure that 'the sight of me may not sully their wives and daughters'. He hoped, however, that future scientists would 'pardon what the vulgar will call my disgusting bestiality' on the grounds that his 'experiment' would help 'in solving the most serious questions in anthropology'.[64]

When the offspring of Mass and the gorilla was born, he was named Hemo, from the Greek word for blood, in order to 'show that he has the blood of man in his apish veins'.[65] However, D'ginna was 'ashamed of having transgressed against the morals of monkeydom with a mere man' and she 'pined for liberty'. D'ginna escaped, taking Hemo with her, but Maas caught up with her just before she was 'swallowed up in a bog'. 'With her last effort', D'ginna threw their son to Maas.[66] He raised the child, carefully recording his observations under the headings 'Hemo-Man' and 'Hemo-Monkey', according to 'which category the hybrid monster most inclines'.[67]

Predictably, both Hemo and Maas came to inglorious ends. Hemo was sold to a member of the Society for the Abolition of the Slave Trade. He ended up playing in a music hall in Amsterdam, where he murdered a love-rival. He was confined to a cage in the Zoological Gardens, which unfortunately burst into flames one evening. Maas rushed to the rescue but Hemo was unable to escape. When Maas fell on his knees crying 'Hemo! My son! My son!', the 'monkey part of Hemo's nature vanishe[d], and the man assert[ed] itself'.[68] Hemo died singing 'his own funeral hymn to Fire'.[69] As for Maas, he became a 'gibbering idiot' and spent the rest of his life in an asylum attempting to 'solve the great problems of religion, the descent of species, and anthropology'.[70]

Roscaud was not only obsessed by stories about interspecies relationships, rape and reproduction. He also told many tales about the abduction of 'negresses' by the 'bad niggers', which he claimed

Title page of *Human Gorillas* (1901), by Count Roscaud.

was what the people of Guinea called gorillas.[71] In one story, Esther (the eighteen-year-old daughter of an English missionary family) was 'violated by a gorilla' and left for dead.[72] Roscaud recalled that the gorilla who had been responsible 'lived by plunder and had strangled more than one negress, though not much notice had been taken of its doings till it carried off Miss Esther'.[73] They slaughtered him.

This hierarchy of sentient species is common in such literature: the ravishment of Black women is less notable than white ones; gorillas are casually massacred.

In conclusion, let us return to Linda Lovelace's heartrending autobiography. In it, male human beings not only equate women with animals but insult a male dog called Norman by forcing him to have sex with a non-consenting Lovelace. The (human) men are little more than 'beasts' themselves, and racist ones as well. Readers are encouraged to question whether the chief conflict in interpersonal relationships is due to irreconcilable genders (female or male) or to different genera (*Canis* or *Homo*). The refusal to grant animals and some humans (women and non-Europeans) respect, autonomy and subjectivity pervades much bestiality literature. Lovelace's autobiography enables us to critique questions of consent and affection. Both she and Norman possess 'lives that matter'. Both were being groomed and coerced into a sexual encounter. Lovelace's autobiography asks: are men animals? Although insulting to real-life animals (including the 'bleary' Norman), her answer is a resounding yes.

Three

Mad or Bad?

Define: **Paraphilia.**
Viz. the Greek prefix 'para' meaning 'besides' and 'philia' meaning 'love'.

Wicked, sinful, immoral: these three words are repeatedly flung at people who even dare to *think* about sex with non-human animals. Those who *act* on their fantasies are 'beastly' or 'bestial', cast down from their elevated position at the crown of God's Creation. From the late nineteenth century, however, a more secular language was increasingly heard: bestiality was being medicalized. As the institutional and ideological power of psychiatry (and, in particular, its forensic branch) grew, people who had sex with non-human animals were increasingly diagnosed with psychiatric disorders.

The most influential commentator driving this change was Austro-German forensic psychiatrist Richard von Krafft-Ebing, whose *Psychopathia Sexualis, with Special Reference to the Antipathic Sexual Instinct: A Medico-forensic Study* was first published in 1886, followed by an English translation ten years later. Between its first publication and Krafft-Ebing's death in 1904, *Psychopathia Sexualis* went through twelve editions. The latest edition was published in 2011, albeit as a historical text rather than a diagnostic guide.

Krafft-Ebing turned 'bestiality' into 'zoophilia' and 'zooerastie'. For him, 'zoophilia' was a kind of fetish that involved a longing (whether sexual or not) for animals, while zooerastie was a pathological form of sexual desire. Through a series of case studies, Krafft-Ebing portrayed people who engaged in sexual acts with

Portrait of Richard von Krafft-Ebing as the frontispiece to the English-language edition of his book *Psychopathia Sexualis* (New York, 1906).

animals as profoundly unpleasant personalities. According to him, they possessed a 'heavy taint' and were suffering from a 'constitutional neurosis' that made them 'impotent for the normal act'. They were atavistic throwbacks to earlier evolutionary stages of life. In other words, bestialists were degenerates. They were vicious and incorrigible. A typical bestialist (according to Krafft-Ebing) was a patient whose unmarried mother was 'deeply tainted' and 'hysteron-epileptic'; the patient's 'deformed, asymmetrical cranium and deformity and asymmetry of the bones of the face' were proof of 'psychical degeneracy'; and he had been a masturbator and abuser of animals since his early youth. In short, the bestialist was a 'human monster'.[1]

Krafft-Ebing's descriptions of brutish men who engaged in sex with animals were profoundly influential. In psychiatric circles, his views were much more likely to be cited than those of other psychiatrists (including Sigmund Freud) who believed that bestialists were simply pathetic men, driven into the embrace of animals because they were either impotent or afraid of female sexuality.[2]

By the early twentieth century, it was common to read in psychiatric and forensic texts that bestialists suffered from an 'impulse obsession' and possessed a 'hereditary degeneracy'.[3] This was the view of forensic physician Léon-Henri Thoinot. When his 1898 lectures to the Faculty of Medicine in Paris were published in English under the title *Medicolegal Aspects of Moral Offenses* (1911), they conjured up the typical bestialist as being a young man who 'had a horror of women' and, from adolescence, engaged in sexual activity with hens, ducks, horses and cows. Thoinot was not surprised to discover that his patient had alcoholic parents, was a mystic and, since childhood, experienced 'epileptic vertigo, followed by brief attacks of ambulatory automatism'.[4] In another one of Thoinot's cases, he described a 'young peasant' who showed both 'physical and moral imperfections'.[5] The peasant

> is short, the trunk is slightly asymmetrical but without marked deformity; the cranium exhibits an abnormal flattening of the right frontal and temporal bony projection, hence a very distinct facial asymmetry; the palatine vault is pointed and the teeth carious.[6]

If that were not bad enough, he was 'addicted to masturbation' and showed no interest in sport. He had a passion for rabbits and at nightfall he goes towards the loft where his employer's rabbits are housed; he seizes a rabbit, kisses it madly; presses it against his body, and in some cases performs coitus . . . The sight of the rabbit and contact with her kindle his desires.[7]

Only in this way could this peasant find relief from an 'atrocious pain in the head' which felt as if 'some one was hammering his cranium with blows from big stones'.[8]

Journalistic accounts of bestialists quickly adopted the sensationalist language of forensic psychiatrists. A significant proportion of these accounts were translations from earlier French or German texts. In 1933, for example, Gaston Dubois-Desaulle's book *Bestiality: An Historical, Medical, Legal, and Literary Study* was released in English, 28 years after it had first been published in French. Although Dubois-Desaulle conceded that some bestialists were more disturbed than others, he never questioned the view that sexual love for a 'beast' was 'a symptom of a mental disease'. It was nothing short of 'an anomaly springing from social pathology, from teratology, from morbid psychology'. In other words, it was a monstrous, constitutional abnormality. Like many commentators, Dubois-Desaulle believed that the sex of the chosen animal was important. Male bestialists who preferred having sex with male animals or who used the 'excremental organs of a female animal' were engaged in 'active pederasty'. This was evidence that they were suffering from a much more serious mental disorder than men who preferred female animals (or, indeed, female bestialists committing the act with a male animal) because in such cases there was 'no inversion but only anomaly in the choice of consort'.[9]

What was the evidence for the existence of major psychiatric disorders among bestialists? For forensic psychiatrists like Krafft-Ebing, support for these conclusions could be found in detailed case studies of patients, all of whom were severely disturbed individuals. Others derived their evidence from psychiatric patients incarcerated

Engraving by Thomas Theodor Heine, used in a brochure for Gaston Dubois-Desaulle, *Bestiality: An Historical, Medical, Legal, and Literary Study, with Addenda* (1934).

in mental hospitals. A 1941 survey of men committed to the Eloise psychiatric hospital in Michigan, for example, found extremely high levels of organic psychosis among bestialists. While 4 per cent of rapists, 27 per cent of homosexuals and 44 per cent of voyeurs in this hospital were diagnosed as psychotic, 71 per cent of male bestialists suffered from this serious disorder.[10] Numerous psychiatrists purported to find evidence that men who engaged in sexual activities with animals were either mentally unhinged or so intellectually subnormal that they were scarcely aware of their actions.[11]

It was less clear *why*: did an underlying mental imbalance lead men to bestiality or did their bestial proclivities drive them insane? The search to identify the precise organic component of bestiality engaged the minds of many psychiatrists. As early as the 1880s, Krafft-Ebing speculated that, since many of his patients were sexually aroused by the smell of animals, perhaps the sexual centres in the brain were in close proximity to those of smell.[12]

Although bestialists were widely pathologized in the psychiatric literature, distinctions were made according to age: youthful bestialists were different from their adult counterparts. While long-standing bestiality carried out by mature men was viewed as clear proof of some underlying mental disorder, boys and young men who only occasionally touched animals in a sexual way were looked upon with almost paternalistic indulgence. Young offenders were viewed as simply ignorant. They could be excused on the grounds that they had been fooled into believing popular lore that bestiality cured venereal disease, was a technique for lengthening the penis or, even more bizarrely, was a way of rehearsing for holy matrimony.[13]

This is not to deny that youthful transgressions had to be nipped in the bud. However, they were considered to be primarily opportunistic and experimental. In part, at least, youthful bestiality was believed to be due to the failure of society to cater to male sexual needs. Even Krafft-Ebing accepted that the 'monstrous and revolting' act of bestiality could be the outcome of 'lack of opportunity for natural indulgences', coupled with 'low morality and great sexual desire'.[14] Indulgent attitudes could be countenanced because physicians believed that these young, naive experimenters were primarily rural dwellers who lacked alternative ways to attain sexual gratification. In the words of a psychiatrist based at the University of Pennsylvania Medical School in 1950, bestialists were adolescent boys living in the countryside who engaged in such behaviour as an 'adaptive expedient of bucolic loneliness'. Their practices were nothing more than 'an experimental adventure' that they 'readily abandoned' on reaching maturity.[15] In other words, they were sexually frustrated young men confined in rural societies where pre-marital sexual activity with fellow humans was not only prohibited but vigorously monitored.[16] According to this way of thinking, male sexuality was like a pressure gauge: denied a human 'outlet', virile, young men were irresistibly driven to seek libidinal relief behind haystacks.

In such small, rural communities, boys discovered engaging in this vice in ways that did not physically injure valuable livestock were probably simply rebuked by their parents or local physicians. Sex education was prescribed. This was the approach taken by Dr Ian Craig, the President of the Association of Police Surgeons of Great Britain, when a schoolboy in his home town of Maldon in the Essex countryside was found to have engaged in sexual intercourse with a heifer. The boy confessed to Craig that he had become 'curious and, more important, frustrated' after attending sex instruction in school. He had 'attempted to enlist the services of several girls of his acquaintance to help him with his homework, but had been rejected'. Therefore, when he witnessed some cattle on a farm 'behaving in an interesting manner', he decided to enlist their help instead. Writing in the official journal of police surgeons,

Craig informed his colleagues of the best way to respond. He advised them to practise fatherly forbearance. After all, despite the offence, the young man was 'a pleasant lad, embarrassed and ashamed by the situation'. All that was needed was 'tactful and sympathetic management', including proper sex education and access to more compliant members of the (human) opposite sex.[17] Rather insensitively, Craig also quipped that when the farmer's wife witnessed the boy dismounting from the rear-end of a cow called the Pride of Hanningfield, she was 'somewhat indignant – the farmer's wife, not the cow'.[18] So long as the animal was not obviously harmed, schoolboy bestiality was misguided, rather than pathological.

Diagnostic Categories

Psychiatric conceptualizations of bestiality underwent a major shift from 1980, however. The driving force behind this change was the inclusion of zoophilia in the third edition of the American Psychiatric Association's *Diagnostic and Statistical Manual of Mental Disorders* (DSM). The DSM was first published in 1952 and has gone through seven editions, culminating in the DSM-5 (2013). It is the official diagnostic manual for American psychiatrists and has been adopted worldwide. It is widely considered to be the psychiatric profession's bible.

Early editions of the DSM included a section entitled 'Sexual Deviations' and typically listed practices such as homosexuality, transvestism, paedophilia, fetishism and sexual sadism.[19] From DSM-III (1980) onwards, however, 'Sexual Deviations' was jettisoned for the less pejorative-sounding term 'Paraphilias', under which a new diagnostic category appeared. This was zoophilia. DSM-III described zoophilia as a psychiatric disorder in which 'the act or fantasy of engaging in sexual activity [with] animals' was a 'repeatedly preferred or exclusive method of achieving sexual satisfaction'.[20] Seven years later, however, the committee responsible for DSM-III-R downgraded its seriousness as a paraphilia, declaring that zoophilia was 'virtually never a clinically significant problem by itself' but was usually associated with other paraphilias, such as paedophilia, voyeurism, exhibitionism and transvestism.[21] By DSM-IV, published in 1994, zoophilia had lost its stand-alone status but was listed under 'Paraphilia Not Otherwise Specified', along with telephone scatologia (an obsession for making obscene telephone calls), necrophilia (engaging in sex with corpses), partialism (exclusive sexual focus on one part of the body), and the three fetishes coprophilia, klismaphilia and urohilia (for faeces, enemas and urine, respectively).[22]

The inclusion of zoophilia in the various editions of the DSM, either as a major paraphilia or as one of numerous other sexual preferences, was contested. Many psychiatrists believed that the DSM's authors had been too restrictive when they insisted that patients had to 'repeatedly' engage in or 'exclusively' prefer sex with animals rather than with humans to be diagnosed with zoophilia. They pointed out that this excluded a large proportion of people who engaged in sexual activities with animals. The DSM's approach also encompassed a vast array of behaviours. Not only did it fail to differentiate between the sex, age and type of animal, for example, but it ignored the very different circumstances and aims of sexual encounters.[23] In other words, it did not differentiate the naive farmhand from the sadistic zoophile who took pleasure in mutilation and murder.

The diagnostic category of zoophilia also became enmeshed in a wider debate about why people could be diagnosed with a paraphilia only if they were distressed or impaired by their sexual practices and/or preferences. This stipulation meant that it was possible to argue that if bestialists were neither hurt, upset nor rendered socially incapacitated by their fantasies or practices, there was no problem. Religious groups were appalled. Along with homosexuality, religious moralists argued that the sexual preference or practice of bestiality was in itself pathological (as well as sinful) and they suspected psychiatrists of legitimating deviant sex.

Yet other critics attacked one of the fundamental premises of the DSM: medicalization. There were furious debates, for example, about the pathologizing of ordinary life experiences, such as grief, and the medicalization of non-normative sexual expression. The fact that early editions of the DSM had identified homosexuality as a 'sexual deviation' or 'paraphilia', listed alongside sexual sadism and bestiality, enraged activists within burgeoning gay rights movements. In part because of their lobbying, members of the American Psychiatric Association voted in 1973 to remove homosexuality from the DSM (although it was retained under the category 'sexual orientation disturbance' until 1987).

The diagnostic category of 'zoophilia' became tangled up in these debates. The sexologist R.E.L. Masters was one of the permissive voices. In *Forbidden Sexual Behavior and Morality: An Objective Re-examination of Perverse Sex Practices in Different Cultures* (1962), Masters confidently asserted that modern scientists, 'basing their opinions upon extensive and impeccable data', generally concluded that 'man's desire to mate with members of species other than his own is quite natural', not pathological. Indeed, he claimed, bestialists were significantly *less* 'perverted' than homosexuals since bestialists 'humanized' their '*opposite*-sex animal love object' while the homosexual's *same*-sex love-object was 'an abnormal one'. In other words, bestialists tended to desire the opposite sex when choosing animal partners – which was less deviant than homosexual love for humans of the same sex. In this, Masters was challenging the views of Krafft-Ebing, who believed that the zooerast was 'farther removed from the normal object' than the homosexual. Masters also drew attention to the fact that 'parallel tendencies' could be 'found among other representatives of the animal world' – in other words, non-human animals also had sex with species other than their own. Negative attitudes towards bestiality, Masters argued, were simply 'emotionalism run amok, magical and theological superstition, puritanism, and hysteria'.[24]

Masters believed that people who engaged in sex with animals were not necessarily 'morbidly abnormal' or even 'abnormally feebleminded'. They were, firstly, 'normally sensual persons without strong inhibitions' against having sex with animals and, secondly, people who 'found themselves in situations where desire coincided with opportunity for gratification by means of bestiality'. There was another, and rather expansive, category of zoophiles according to Masters. This third category included 'jaded voluptuaries' (or people devoted to sensual experiences), 'highly imaginative individuals for whom bestiality is an esthetic as well as an erotic experience', the 'sexually amoral' and, finally, 'curious individuals for whom the act . . . serve[s] an educational purpose'.[25] Masters insisted that bestialists were more likely to be intellectually *superior* humans – an argument that was fundamentally at odds with earlier generations of forensic commentators who believed that people who sought sexual gratification with animals were degenerates or congenitally inferior specimens of humanity.

Masters's 'permissive' view of bestiality even led him to endorse the 'grooming' of animals for sex. Masters informed readers that 'the animal's response is far more likely to be an erotic one if, as is the case with human females, it has been subjected beforehand to a lengthy period of caresses and what may be called "love play".' He argued that the bestialist must '"woo" the chosen sex-object, in order to allay anxieties, and in order to bring that object to pitch of erotic arousal similar to his own'. In a particularly disturbing passage, Masters contended that this initial stage of wooing need not continue throughout the relationship. 'Like women', he maintained, animals

> respond to competent erotic training by becoming conditioned eventually to an increasingly swift response to the needs of the

sex partner, so that 'love play' need not be so prolonged as when the animal was still a novice to the zoophilic relationship.

In another offensive paragraph, Masters maintained that animals react to being raped 'even less satisfactorily, and often with more vigorous resistance . . . than women'.[26] This candid dismissal of the libidinal needs of females of both human and non-human species characterized his discussions of zoophilia.

Mental Illness

Although Masters was one of the leading sexologists of the permissive 1960s subculture, his views were not widely embraced. A formidable range of psychiatrists began publishing research purporting to show that bestialists and zoophiles were mentally ill. For example, William A. Alvarez and Jack P. Freinhar examined sixty psychiatric inpatients, medical inpatients and psychiatric staff members. They found that 55 per cent of the psychiatric patients had either engaged in sexual acts with animals or fantasized about doing so, compared with only 15 per cent of psychiatric staff and 10 per cent of medical patients. While none of the staff or non-psychiatric inpatients had ever actually had sex with an animal, nearly one-third of psychiatric patients had done so.[27]

Even the antics of 'naive' adolescents started to be scrutinized for signs of a much more alarming malaise than mere curiosity or frustration. A tsunami of psychiatric and psychological research centred primarily on urban adolescents and young men suggested that those who engaged in sexual practices with animals were suffering from severe mental illnesses. Other psychiatric surveys studied young men who were either in psychiatric or correctional facilities. For example, a study published in the *Journal of Forensic Psychiatry* in 1998 found that 10 per cent of juvenile sex offenders within a psychiatric facility had engaged in sex with animals.[28]

A similar study based at three juvenile institutions in the Midwest revealed that over 6 per cent of 381 male youths reported at least one sexual act with an animal.[29]

These offenders were believed to be not only seriously mentally ill, but highly dangerous. Based on detailed case notes relating to individual zoophiles, psychiatrists such as Gene G. Abel (author of the controversial Abel Assessment for Sexual Interest, a sexual offender assessment tool), along with psychologists such as Judith V. Becker, Jerry Cunningham-Rathner and Joanne L. Rouleau, began warning fellow medical professionals, criminologists and legal experts that men convicted of sexual offences with animals were 'the most deviant and indiscriminate of sex offenders'.[30]

Their main contention was that people who engaged in cruel acts against animals would also be callous in their dealings with people. It became routine to claim that bestialists resembled child sexual offenders. Links were made between men who consumed child and animal pornography: both kinds of pornography were distributed via websites specializing in sexual deviance and both types of offenders sexualized patterns of domination.[31] Even extremely young bestialists were dangerous: children who sexually abused animals were deemed highly likely to sexually abuse other children as well. In one study, 10 per cent of children referred to a tertiary centre for being sexual abusers had engaged in zoophilic behaviours.[32] As two psychiatrists concluded in a 1991 article published in the *International Journal of Psychosomatics*,

> The zoophile's world is similar to the rapist's and child sexual abuser's. They all view the physical gratification they have with their victims as consensual, and they believe it benefits their partners as well as themselves.

They claimed that both paedophiles and zoophiles make a distinction between men who abuse and those who love their object of desire, making great efforts to 'plac[e] themselves, of course, in the latter group'.[33]

This post-1980s alarm about the dangerousness of people who had sex with animals also insisted that bestialists had a tendency to commit aggressive crimes. In a study of adult men in an Iowa prison, one in nine (11 per cent) had witnessed or committed a sexual act with an animal.[34] Another survey found that 14 per cent of inmates in Southern correctional institutions had engaged in bestiality.[35] Investigations of men incarcerated in maximum- and medium-security correctional institutions found levels of bestiality ranging from 6 to 13 per cent.[36] Criminologists such as Chris Hensley and his colleagues, who published their research in the *International Journal of Offender Therapy and Comparative Criminology*, contended that bestiality was 'most often found among violent offenders, sexual offenders, and those individuals who have themselves been sexually abused'. It was an 'apparent precursor for later recurrent violent crimes'.[37] Dozens of other psychiatrists, psychologists, criminologists and social workers concurred that zoophiles had a particularly high likelihood of 'dangerousness'.[38]

Like their predecessors in the late nineteenth and earlier twentieth centuries, these commentators were less clear about *why* people engaged in such behaviours. Speculations proliferated. Perhaps zoophilia was a form of species dysphoria or 'living in the wrong body', like transsexualism.[39] Maybe zoophiles were simply unable to communicate effectively with other sentient beings.[40] Fearing rejection, they might become isolated from other humans.[41] A study entitled 'Criminal Histories of a Subsample of Animal Cruelty Offenders' (2016) reported that zoophiles maintained that animal sex 'provided freedom from entangling cares and civilized pretense that they had experienced in human sexual contact'. For these men, sex with animals was 'simple, straightforward': they didn't have to 'barter' or invest time or money.[42] With the rise of neuropsychiatry in the late twentieth and early twenty-first centuries, speculations about whether sexually perverted men were actually suffering some kind of organic brain deformation grew. In 2002, for example, three scientists writing in the journal *Psychiatry Research: Neuroimaging* examined the brain of an elderly man who had a history of bestiality, paedophilia, exhibitionism and transvestism. This patient was found to have significant atrophy of his hippocampus, compared with the brains of other patients who had died in the same institution but had not suffered from any sexual perversion.[43] These scientists admitted that extrapolating a causal link from the brain of one man was imprudent, but the mystery of zoo urges drove them to speculate.

Cure?

Was there a cure for zoophilia? Treatments were extremely variable. Fairly benign forms included behaviourist-orientated 'satiation', 'covert sensitization' and 'stimulus control' treatments. These were the treatments used on 'Mr Z', a patient diagnosed with 'zoophilic exhibitionism'. Mr Z's only form of sexual expression was masturbating in front of large dogs of either sex and peeping through the windows of homes where large dogs lived. When asked how he thought the dogs felt about his activities, he claimed that they 'probably enjoyed it'.[44] Curiously, Mr Z never attempted to engage in penetrative acts with any of the dogs; he did not even fantasize about doing so.

Two behaviourists – Richard McNally and Brian Lukach – decided to treat him through satiation. This meant that Mr Z had to

> masturbate to orgasm while verbalizing nondeviant fantasies (e.g. sexual intercourse with a woman), and then continue to masturbate postorgasmically for 30 minutes while repeatedly verbalizing the most exciting component of the deviant image (e.g. ejaculating in the dog's face).

This was expected to 'enhance the erotic value of nondeviant cues, while rendering deviant ones boring'. They explained that

> The rationale is Pavlovian: nondeviant cues become established as appetitive conditioned stimuli, whereas deviant cures undergo Pavlovian extinction through nonreinforcement.[45]

Mr Z carried out this conditioning in the privacy of his home between three and five times a week for five months. His masturbatory sessions were even recorded to ensure that he was actually doing it. The scientists reported that 'not only did he exhibit 100% compliance, but he insisted that we checked the tapes because he was anxious to know whether he was "doing it right".'[46] In the final three months of his treatment, they introduced covert sensitization. In the context of the clinic, Mr Z was asked to describe (in thirty seconds) an 'activity that had commonly preceded deviant behavior (e.g., wandering through the neighborhood in search of dogs)', followed by describing (for ninety seconds) an 'aversive scene describing a realistic consequence of offending (e.g., being fired from his job)'. These descriptions were taped and replayed by Mr Z at home throughout the next few weeks.[47] The final part of his treatment was labelled 'stimulus control'. Mr Z was encouraged to reflect on the chain of events, including his moods and thoughts, that facilitated his behaviour. He was then 'helped to generate alterative behaviors', including ways to avoid risky situations. The scientists noted that 'high risk situations included unstructured leisure time, periods when his grandmother was not at home, and places where people were not present.' Armed with this knowledge, Mr Z was

> counseled to take busy routes when going on errands rather than to take short cuts where he might encounter stray dogs with no

one else present. He was instructed to set his alarm clock so that he had just enough time to get ready for work.[48]

Mr Z was lucky. Other relatively benign treatments included group and family therapy, avoidance techniques, psychotherapy and training. But not all forms of treatment were so painless. Many were extremely harsh. They included drugs and electric shock treatment, not to mention incarceration.[49]

Problems

The problem with much of this clinical research is that it was carried out on populations that were highly marginalized in the first place. Practically all the studies based their analyses on men (and, very rarely, women) who were either incarcerated in prison for serious acts of violence or had been committed to mental institutions on the grounds of long-standing psychiatric problems. Given such samples, it was inevitable that these forensic specialists would conclude that bestiality was a symptom of violent criminal tendencies, psychosis and other serious mental afflictions.[50] There is actually little evidence that zoophilia is a 'reliable risk factor for prediction of sexual offenses against humans'.[51]

'Sampling bias' was one problem; another was that commentators linking zoophilia with sexual dangerousness often drew their evidence from evaluations made by social workers and psychologists employed in Sexually Violent Predator court hearings.[52] From the 1980s, many U.S. legislatures introduced Sexually Violent Predator laws (SVP), sometimes known as Sexually Dangerous Predator laws. They were passed in the context of widespread public panic about sexually violent men who committed new offences on being released from prison. The laws mandated indefinite 'inpatient, civil psychiatric commitment for individuals who have completed their prison sentence for a sexually violent crime, have a diagnosed mental disorder, and are deemed likely to repeat'.[53] The difference with the earlier psychopath laws is that offenders committed under SVP laws served their prison sentences, *after* which they were committed to a secure hospital. 'In all but name', this meant imprisonment, often for life.[54] The most common diagnosis for people committed under SVP laws was paedophilia, followed by Paraphilias 'Not Otherwise Specified', which, as mentioned earlier, was the usual diagnosis for zoophiles. The problem is that much of the evidence linking bestiality or zoophilia with sexual dangerousness came from social workers and psychologists evaluating men under SVP laws. In other words, they were biased towards making links between deviance and dangerousness. Only rarely were commentators willing to acknowledge such biases. One exception was the authors of a study who admitted the possibility that 'among other populations (single women and their pets) . . . sex acts with animals might be performed out of love, the need for consolation, or other motivations.'[55]

In addition, zoo dysfunctionality might have been due to societal attitudes to their desires rather than to the existence of a paraphilia. Zoophiles were often ostracized by wider society; loneliness was endemic. Many (if not most) suffered from low self-esteem; they complained of bouts of depression and lived in constant fear of being 'outed'. In other words, mental illness might have been the result and not the cause of their bestial urges.

A poignant example of this can be found in a remarkable autobiography written by a Missouri man named Mark Matthews, a lover of horses. In it Matthews described in tortuous detail the way he struggled to understand and accept his sexual desire for everything equine. While at university, he sought out as much literature as he could find about zoophilia and even consulted a counsellor about it. However, as his 'treatment' proceeded, he became further and further confused, convinced that I must be some sort of cosmic screw-up, human garbage. I became a recluse, seldom leaving my residence hall except to work a student job in the computational center . . . I attempted suicide once, taking a whole bottle of over-the-counter sleeping pills . . . Another time, during a weekend at home, I stared for a long hour down the barrel of a loaded shotgun, thumb on the trigger, mentally flipping a coin to decide whether or not to press it.[56]

I will return to Matthews's life story in the next chapter, but his heart-rending feelings of isolation due to his interspecies affections are probably far more typical of zoosexual lives than any of the reports focusing on imprisoned or incarcerated 'bestialists'. He was fortunate in that he found a community of 'electronic friends' with whom he could correspond anonymously. On the computer, Matthews wrote,

You were safe. If no one knew you, no one could hate you for what you really were, for your dark, hidden side. It was all just electrons, photon-image ripples flowing across a screen. Those couldn't hurt you, stab you in the back after you made yourself vulnerable.[57]

In fact, Matthews might have been in a stronger social position than most zoophiles because at least his parents and, eventually, friends accepted his minority sexual preference.[58]

Along with other zoophiles, Matthews argued strongly that sexual acts with animals could encourage closer communication between sexual partners, as well as a recognition that they were complex, emotional beings, rather than merely means to a libidinal end. Indeed, rather than assuming that love for animals was inferior to the love of humans or was a substitution for 'real' relationships, there is evidence that people who have strong bonds with animals also have strong social bonds with other people.[59] The argument 'cruel to animals, ergo cruel to humans' is also based on a narrow definition of sexuality – that is, an aggressive, penetrative model. In other words, the love of animals could stimulate greater love towards humans. This is exactly what zoophiles like Matthews attempted to do, as we shall see in the next chapter.

Four

'Zoo' Communities

Define: **Sexual Orientation.**
A person's sense of individual and community identity based
on patterns of intellectual, emotional and sexual attraction
to an 'Other'.

Mark Matthews's *The Horse-man: Obsessions of a Zoophile*
(1994) was part-memoir, part-fiction. It is a searing
account of human–horse love. For people not previously aware
that there existed a sexual orientation called zoosexuality, it
quickly catapulted him into the spotlight. He became one of
the most vocal voices in the zoo movement. In January 1992
Matthews founded ZOO, the Zoophiliac Outreach Organization,
which offered 'nonprofessional peer-group advice and mutual
support' for 'zoos', as they called themselves.[1] Two years later,
he hosted the first 'zoo conference' – called ZooCon – from
his trailer, an event that was followed a few months later by
'ZooGathering', convened in a Holiday Inn in New Mexico.[2]
Matthews also regularly appeared in films exploring zoo identities.
In 1999, for example, he appeared in a British Channel Four
documentary, directed by C. Spencer and produced by Simon
Andreae, entitled *Hidden Sex: Animal Passions*.[3] He also appeared
in Robinson Devor's 2007 film *Zoo*.

Matthews was a deeply flawed man, but his love for individual
ponies was unmistakable. In particular, 'Cherry' had a personality,
as well as a sexed body, that he found attractive.[4] When he finally
allowed himself to love Cherry, he found immense pleasure and
reciprocal satisfaction in their life together. He described how

They made slow love, using their whole bodies in foreplay, rubbing against each other, caressing with hands, lips, noses, teeth, using all that each had to use; then, when his testicles and penis ached with arousal, he entered her and they rocked on their feet in blissful harmony . . . 'I love you, little girl. I'm *in love with* you. You're so sweet, so funny, so – oh, Cherry, my darling!' He hugged her neck, hung her head over his shoulder, rubbing his cheek against her sleek coat.[5]

Such passages – replete with cliché and soft-porn mannerism – occur throughout Matthews's memoir. Despite the lack of literary flair, the emotions Matthews was struggling to convey were real enough.

Indeed, the memoir is less an attempt to create a literary classic, and more a chronicle of one man's journey to self-realization and self-acceptance. He went into a period of deep mourning after Cherry died, but eventually found love again with an older mare named Dottie. In 1990, however, an accident destroyed all sexual functions. As he bluntly put it: 'no erections, no orgasms, no ejaculation.'[6] However, he continued,

> I have learned that sex and love don't always require orgasms to be satisfying. Just being close, being coupled, touching, smooching, trading caresses with lips, tongue, and hands can be wonderful. Sitting in my easy chair in the living room with two cats in my lap and Dottie standing alongside (she's naturally housebroken), watching television or listening to music, I feel a warmth and companionship that I can trust. No games, no power plays, just honest affection.[7]

He dismissed claims that he was engaging in anthropomorphic fantasies. Dottie 'is a horse. She acts and reacts as a horse.'[8] And that is why he loved her.

Mark Matthews and Pixel on *The Jerry Springer Show*, in a 1992 episode titled 'I Married a Horse'.

Matthews was clearly influenced in his ideas by John Money, the famous sexologist from Johns Hopkins University who specialized in questions of gender identity. Money is even thanked in his autobiography. Like Money, Matthews argued that zoophilia was a kind of 'species dysphoria', comparable (in his view) to the gender dysphoria affecting transsexuals.[9] He was keen to point out that the zoophiles he met were 'all functional members of society' and came from all walks of life. He noted that

> A few doctors here and there suggest that we need a 'cure' for our inclinations. By contrast, few suggest trying to 'cure' homosexuality anymore – it has even been removed from the standard lists of paraphilias.

Other physicians prescribed drugs such as lithium or Depo-Provera for men and women with a zoosexual orientation – perhaps such medications would help by reducing the zoo's 'sex drive' so they could 'control what is viewed as a compulsion'.[10] Matthews believed that such treatments were inappropriate because they treated zoophilia 'as a mere sexual outlet, ignoring its emotional component'.[11] He insisted that he would 'rather see the medical community offer these people assistance towards self-acceptance and better methods of interfacing with a society that rarely understands their problems'.[12]

Matthews not only contended that zoophilia was a 'normal' sexual orientation, but maintained that zoosexuals had a great deal to offer society more broadly. Zoophiles could teach people who possessed more conventional sexual orientations how to better communicate with each other and their environments. Loving animals, Matthews argued, could encourage love for people. In his words, 'I feel I am a better person for my choice [of love object] than I was before, able to appreciate people as people rather than as sex objects or rivals.' His first pony-lover, Cherry, 'taught me I *could*, after everything that had happened in my life, love' while his last, Dottie, 'taught me *how much* I would love'.[13]

Sexual Identity

Matthews's account of being a zoophile was important in generating academic interest in such alternative sexual communities. Crucially, researchers from the same disciplines that had been responsible for the pathologization of bestialists – that is, the psychiatrists, sexologists and sociologists we explored in the last chapter – began revising their views. Rather than basing their assessments on men incarcerated in high-security prisons or psychiatric hospitals, as the previous generation of researchers had done, they met with zoophiles like Matthews and began actively engaging with members of zoo communities. To their own surprise, many of these researchers found themselves in sympathy with the people they met.

Five studies have been most insightful. One of the earliest was carried out by sexologist Hani Miletski, who had a reputation for being willing to take on 'edgy' projects, having previously published work on incest between mothers and sons.[14] Her original reserve about zoophiles became more supportive when she realized that 'these people are perfectly fine . . . They just like to do what they do.' She recognized that there was nothing 'wrong with them. So I started to change my perception,' increasingly recognizing that zoophilia was 'a sexual orientation' rather than a perversion.[15] Miletski's research subjects were 82 male and 11 female zoophiles, all of whom responded to a 23-page-long questionnaire, which included open-ended questions such as 'Is there anything else you would like to share?' Her results were published in the *Journal of Sex Education and Therapy* in 2001.[16]

Similar methodologies were adopted by the other researchers I will be focusing on in this chapter. Psychologist Andrea Beetz collected data from 114 men and 3 women in addition to conducting detailed interviews with a smaller group. In 2003 the sociologists Colin J. Williams and Martin S. Weinberg also immersed themselves within a zoophilic community, publishing their results in *Archives of Sexual Behavior*. Finally, Damian Jacob Sendler published two studies, one with Michal Lew-Starowicz. One of Sendler's studies was entitled 'Why People Who Have Sex with Animals Believe That It Is Their Sexual Orientation' (2018), and involved him undertaking a search of Internet forums dealing with zoophiles, and then conducting thematic analyses of the responses of 121 men and 17 women.[17] His paper with Lew-Starowicz broadened this analysis to include 245 zoophiles.[18]

What is remarkable about these studies is the high degree of similarity they describe in terms of the profile of participants, their motivations and their practices. Up to 90 per cent of the male zoos and all of the female ones expressed a preference for small animals, particularly dogs.[19] Zoos engaged in a wide variety of sexual acts. In

Miletski's survey 64 per cent of the men and women masturbated a dog, between 42 and 45 per cent performed fellatio on the dog, over half (55 per cent) of the women had the dog perform cunnilingus on them, one-third of the men had the dog penetrate them anally, and over half (55 per cent) of the women were vaginally penetrated by the dog.[20] Although there were significant differences in how often these zoophiles had sex with their chosen animal, on average, zoo sex took place two to three times a week.[21]

The personal characteristics of the zoophiles in these surveys varied. None of the researchers mention ethnicity, but it is highly likely that the vast majority were white Europeans or Americans. They ranged in age between 19 and 78, with an average age in the mid- to late thirties.[22] Almost half were college graduates.[23] It was notable that they did not seem particularly exceptional in terms of personality. Beetz, for example, observed that while zoos experienced slightly higher levels of interpersonal difficulties compared to non-zoos, in general they 'had the same degree or fewer signs of psychopathy, were more sympathetic and helpful than most people, and had a typical need for control and dominance'.[24]

There was greater heterogeneity when it came to the range and nature of their sexual relationships. One-quarter of the zoophiles in Beetz's study had never had a sexual experience with a human, one-quarter were not interested in sex with humans, and 57 per cent maintained that sex with animals was more important than sex with humans.[25] More than three-quarters told Beetz that their relationships with animals were 'like the relationships they have with a human partner'.[26] In contrast, Miletski found that almost half of her zoophiles were not in a relationship with a human at the time of the survey. A small number claimed to be married to their animal while others reported that their animal was a 'mate'.[27] Unlike Beetz's sample, 73 per cent of the women and just over half of the men that Miletski talked to also had sexual intercourse with humans of the opposite sex: one woman and 29 men (36 per cent of the men) had sexual relations with a human of the same sex.[28] This was more in line with Sendler and Lew-Starowicz's survey. Almost half of the zoophiles they surveyed only had sex with animals. One-quarter were in committed and openly acknowledged relationships with human as well as animal partners (a practice known as 'fence jumping').[29] Of the 17 per cent of zoophiles who claimed to be in a committed relationship with a human partner only, nearly half nevertheless regularly engaged in sexual intercourse with animals. One-quarter had not told their human partner of this form of sexual activity.[30]

Given that all of these researchers contacted participants via zoophilic websites, it is not surprising that they were committed to the idea that zoophilia was a sexual orientation rather than a form of deviancy. Emboldened by the success of gay liberation, these websites explicitly modelled themselves along the lines employed by homosexual activists and, more recently, transgender ones.[31] Before turning their interest to zoophiles, Williams and Weinberg had conducted research with homosexuals and so were particularly well placed to observe the similarities between the early gay communities that they studied in the 1960s and '70s and zoophilic ones at the end of the twentieth and beginning of the twenty-first centuries.[32] Both groups spoke of their sexuality in terms of 'forbidden love'. They did not want to be 'cured' and they repeatedly told researchers that 'acceptance of their bestiality and zoophilia is the most important factor for their sense of well-being.'[33]

Zoos believed that their sexual relations with animals was 'innate'.[34] As one female zoophile recalled, well before she understood anything about 'sex, sexuality, morality, or zoophilia', she recognized that she had 'a deep love for animals, a bond that was undeniable'. She did not 'choose' to be a zoosexual: 'It is just a part of who and what I am – one part of many. It is natural, consensual, satisfying, and overwhelmingly loving. My dogs are happy – I am happy.'[35] It was a sentiment echoed by another zoophile. 'I feel a draw to dogs,' he maintained, adding that his attraction was to 'Rottweiler above all other breeds. It's as if I am a Rottweiler, but I have the body of a human.'[36] This kind of 'species dysphoria' was tied up with debates about 'nature' and 'natural'. Half of Sendler's sample, for example, believed that it was not possible to know what 'nature wants' (except in evolutionary terms), by which they meant that no one had the right to say that zoophilia was 'unnatural'. After all, his respondents maintained, zoophilia had 'persisted through time'. This was proof, if any were needed, that 'nature', in the 'process of evolution', made some people 'inclined to engage in the act of sex with animals'. Humans were 'part of the animal kingdom' and so, 'by extension, any sexual activity that occurs within that framework of the natural world is biologically ascribed – and natural (= normal).'[37] A particularly determinist version of this was espoused by one zoosexual, who informed Sendler that

> There is no God. Only the law of genetics. As we are born, the blueprints for the people we shall become are laid out. Our control over reality is an illusion. Our neurons will fire and our brains will behave as it is programmed regardless of what we do. The choices we make, the beliefs we have, the way we view the world, it is all predetermined by our genetics and our past experiences.

He likened life to being 'on a train, going in one direction, no way off and no way to escape'.[38]

It was a lonely journey, however. All the studies revealed high levels of desolation, guilt, anxiety and depression. Nearly one-quarter of the zoophiles in Miletski's study admitted to having attempted suicide.[39] Many more succeeded. Because zoophiles were vilified for being sexual deviants, all experienced some level of psychological maladjustment. Secrecy was paramount.[40] They could not even feel confident about seeking help from psychiatrists or other mental health specialists.[41] While 57 per cent of zoosexuals were or had been in psychotherapy, only half had told their therapists of their sexual proclivities.[42] Those who did disclose this information often reported that their therapists reacted negatively.[43] Both male and female zoophiles, however, were keen to distinguish themselves from 'bestialists', whom they castigated for being concerned primarily with 'human gratification'.[44] Indeed, over one-third of the participants in Beetz's study reported being active in animal protection organizations.[45] Many more complained about being stigmatized by being placed in the same category as paedophiles. This was not helped when the North American Man/Boy Love Association (a vocal pro-paedophile group) proclaimed their solidarity with zoophiles.[46] Indeed, according to Sendler's survey at least, one-fifth of the male zoophiles and 6 per cent of the female zoophiles did have paedophilic urges.[47]

Partly in an attempt to defend themselves and partly in solidarity with other zoos, various zoophilic organizations were established. In the mid-1990s, for example, the First Church of Zoophilia, run by 'Pastor Lykaon', was established to offer eternal salvation to people who venerated their 'sacred animals'. The church believes that zoophiles were a persecuted religious minority. They even performed marriage ceremonies between humans and animals. Their argument that zoos (like polygamists) had a constitutional right to freedom of religion was rejected by the courts.

ZETA, or Zoophiles for the Ethical Treatment of Animals (it is perhaps more accurately translated as Zoophiles United for Tolerance and Understanding), was more successful. It was initially set up in America, but by the 1990s it was largely based in Germany. In Berlin on 1 February 2013, ZETA held the first march for zoophilic rights in Berlin. As part of Zoophile Rights Day (ZRD) they hosted a discussion, chaired by Stefanie Unsleber (a reporter at the *TAZ* newspaper), Oliver Burdinski (a zoophile who lived with a pure-bred Siberian husky called Joey), Patrick Drohn (a zoophile) and Dr Lothar Riemenschneider (a sex therapist).[48] They argued that animals were sexual beings and that human zoophilia was a sexual preference, like any other: in other words, zoos should not be apologetic. In an interview Burdinski was frank about the issue of consent. 'A dog cannot speak to you like a human being,' he admitted, adding,

> but they can clearly show what they like and don't like, whether they are hungry, whether they enjoy being touched . . . They can also show whether or not they want to have sexual intercourse. Mounting is not merely a sign of domination, but also a sign of sexual desire . . . we [him and Joey] are not having sex at the moment because Joey does not want to do so and I respect that.[49]

The leadership of ZETA went so far as to report sadistic zoos to the police. As Burdinski recalled, 'we do not tolerate people causing harm to animals.' When they 'became aware of a man in Sweden who had filmed himself raping and murdering a dog' they 'traced his IP address and reported him to the Swedish authorities. He was sentenced to two and a half years in jail.'[50]

ZETA complained that 'the rights of our minority' have been 'severely curtailed' by the re-criminalization of sex between animals and humans. There has been a wave of persecution of zoophiles led by a jittery coalition between right-wing extremists and animal rights activists. Swastikas were painted on their homes; vigils were held outside buildings they frequented; they were sent hate mail and received death threats. ZETA's aim, therefore, was to 'stand up for the rights of zoophiles and to act as a mediator between the zoophiles and state and society'. ZETA declared that

> We zoophiles have always been a part of society and it always will be. We do not disappear, even if you are silent about us or criminalize [us]. We need a common solution to existing problems. And to find them, a dialogue must take place. We are ready.[51]

It was a striking statement of defiance as well as solidarity with fellow zoos. With the increasing backlash against 'permissiveness', along with the rise of animal rights liberationists, ZETA failed to flourish. Having sex with animals was criminalized in Germany in July 2013. Today, as Michael Kiok, one of its leaders, admitted in an interview with me, it is a small movement.[52]

Consent

Questions of how to ascertain willingness to engage in sexual activities with non-human animals loomed large in the minds of zoophiles. It annoyed them that non-zoos routinely exploited animals and were unconcerned by the fact that animals were unable to verbalize their protest, yet at the same time obsessively demanded that zoos obtained spoken consent when talking about sexual relations. Sendler and Lew-Starowicz's survey of zoophilic websites found at least forty discussion threads devoted to how to gauge animal consent.[53] While some zoophiles took their lead from BDSM (bondage, discipline, dominance and submission and sadomasochism) enthusiasts, most shared their own experiences in reading animals' body language, particularly audible and visual cues such as barking, licking and 'looking happy'.[54] Similar to human–human couplings, zoos maintained that animals often 'develop a specific language that only the two parties can understand'.[55] They observed that their chosen lover had 'very specific signs indicating consent, such as bringing a specific toy they normally do not use for playing'.[56] As one zoophile explained,

> My dog will always make a strange little bark and will always try to lick my feet, or my head, with a very slight lick; then lay on his back, continuing with that little bark, until I respond. If I do respond, he will either jump on me and fuck me like crazy, or he will turn his back to me, wanting me to do the same to him.[57]

The role of animals in actively soliciting sex is also a major theme in the autobiographical accounts by zoophiles cited in Masters's *Sex-driven People* (1966).[58]

Crucially, zoos admitted that consent in an animal companion could never be assumed. For example, one zoophile was devastated when his long-term sexual dog companion died. After an extended period of grief, he bought a puppy and waited for her to mature before making sexual advances. When the dog showed no interest in 'having sex with him', he equally 'lost interest in having sex' with her.[59] Proponents of human–animal sexual relations contended that their sexual responses to their animal companion were both loving and reciprocal. Take the case of Malcolm Brenner, who fell in love with a bottle-nosed dolphin called Dolly who lived at a park in south Florida in the 1970s.[60] Brenner claimed that the sex was not only consensual but was initiated by Dolly. In his words,

> When I got into the water with her, she would approach me, unafraid. She would solicit attention. I never fed her, never gave her food or rewards. Her courtship, as it progressed, got more vigorous and intense. She would rub her genital slit against me, and if I tried to push her away, she would get very angry with me.

He confessed that he

> felt very embarrassed. I was not comfortable with my own zoosexuality – I didn't want to be a zoophile . . .
> It took her literally about 3 or 4 months to begin to win me over and convince me that she was intellectually pretty much my equal.[61]

To people who accused him of being a rapist, Brenner reminded them that

Malcolm J. Brenner and Dolly in 1971.

You can't outswim a dolphin in the water . . . We spent half an hour in courtship. If it had been rape it would have been easy for her to stay in the pen where the male dolphins would have protected her from me. Instead, she chose to squeeze between a couple of boards into another pen where we had some privacy. And what she wanted to do was make love to me.[62]

Indeed, animals have been known to 'forsake intercourse with their own kind in testimony to their preference for relations with humans'.[63] To critics who claimed that these animals have been 'groomed' to be responsive to human sexual advances, zoophiles insisted this was not the case. Mutual pleasure was their primary goal. As one zoophile told Miletski, 'I enjoy it very much, so do the animals.' He lamented the fact that 'It can be a bit frustrating that the majority of society has yet to emerge from the ethical Dark Ages and still believe that we are somehow nasty individuals.'

He was confident about the rightness of his 'own ethical code', which he had 'no desire to give up . . . and which does no harm to anyone else'.[64] Nearly three-quarters of zoophiles in one study saw nothing wrong in their sex with animals.[65] In fact, despite high levels of dysfunction and isolation, 69 per cent of men and 82 per cent of the women in Miletski's study reported being 'pretty happy' with their personal life and 93 per cent did not want to stop having sex with animals.[66] This process was helped immeasurably by the establishment of safe, online forums where zoos could communicate with like-minded men and women. The Internet proved to be crucial not only in the establishment of a 'zoo identity' but in sharing information and discussing questions of consent.[67]

Zoo desires evoked strong emotions of affection, incited erotic passion and fulfilled deeply rooted fantasies.[68] Some claimed that animals were 'better lovers'.[69] In Sendler and Lew-Starowicz's study nearly 90 per cent reported that that they found the animal's 'husky smell' to be a significant aspect of their attractiveness: 'the more wet, hairy, and smelly', the more attractive the animal.[70] As Matthews contended, his sexual drives were fuelled by 'the memory of musky earthen scents, flowing tails, firm equine buttocks, and the feel of horsehair against his naked thighs'.[71] Most admitted that they engaged in sex because they were 'sexually attracted to the animal' or 'wanted to express love or affection to the animal'.[72] In other words, zoos were not only seeking sexual contact, but emotional attachments as well. This was especially true for women in the community. A 1982 study of 27 men and 24 women aged between

17 and 28 who had been engaged in bestiality for an average of 5.8 years found that the men were most likely to claim that they were motivated by 'sexual expressiveness' and were least likely to claim to be motivated by 'emotional involvement'. This priority was inverted when female zoos ranked their motivations.[73] In the words of Sarah, speaking about her relationship with a dog called Miles:

> I didn't really become aware of zoophilia until much later in my life . . . When Miles and I moved into my room together, it became a little more intimate. The first time that I actually decided to take my clothes off and feel his fur next to my bare skin was pretty surprising . . . I stripped and lay down on my bed and Miles came up and the two of us just laid down and took a nap together. And I remember waking and I had my arms around him and his paws were up on my shoulder, we were nose to nose, and, you know, I'd wake up and he gave me a lick on my nose and it was just like a regular relationship and just feeling the comfort of his warm body next to mine and it just never felt like anything was wrong in that.

His presence gave her 'pure happiness' that 'has never been equaled'.[74] These gender differences will become important later when I suggest that heteronormative, masculine models of sexuality may not be the most fulfilling ones.

Zoophiles were passionately concerned for 'the animals' welfare and pleasure' and placed a strong 'emphasis on consent in the pursuit of sexual gratification'.[75] Indeed, all the zoos interviewed by Williams and Weinberg claimed to have strong bonds of love for their animal partner and believed that their animal companions loved them in return.[76] In the words of one zoophile, 'My relationship with animals is a loving one in which sex is an extension of that love as it is with humans, and I do not have sex with a horse unless it consents.'[77] Or, as another contended, 'Although I do get an erection when interacting sexually with a stallion, my first priority is always the animal's pleasure, erection, and personal affection toward me.'[78] Zoophiles argue that

> being in a relationship with an animal implies having feelings for their partner, exhibiting emotions that show they care, and engaging in actions that show the pet that they are loved (both sexually and nonsexual, i.e., going on trips).[79]

Many believed that they had a romantic attachment to their animal that was comparable to human love.[80] Indeed, 42 per cent even reported feeling jealousy when their animal lover showed attention to another creature.[81] In the words of one highly educated zoophile who lived with his two 'mare-wives', 'life's good' with his two companions. He took great pleasure seeing them when he awoke every morning and at night he delighted in their company. He just wanted to 'stroke them or hold them or be with them'. They had brought him peace and love – both things he had previously lacked. He admitted that he had

> walked a long, hard road, largely without a map and I took some wrong turns, I had pain and despair and helplessness, but in the end I found the right path, reached my destination and now I am happy and at peace.[82]

Animals could be true partners as well as companion species.

Problems

The zoophiles who have attracted the attention of these sexologists, sociologists and psychologists are not representative of people who have sex with animals. These researchers' samples are just as skewed as those of their predecessors, which focused on prison populations and people with psychiatric disorders. Members of zoophilic communities are likely to be older, more highly educated and with a stronger orientation towards community than other people who have sex with animals. They are more likely to value animals and therefore are more concerned with arguments about and evidence for 'consent' and 'pleasure'. The remarkable similarities in the arguments zoosexuals use to bolster their orientations and practices also suggest a considerable degree of learned advocacy.

It is important to remember that all bestialists and many zoophiles treat their sexual partners as of no intrinsic value or worth. Even if not involving obvious coercion or abuse, zoo practices often view the animal as an object like any other desirable sex-play item, such as a dildo or handcuffs.[83] The animal lover may be nothing more than a 'release' from the pressures of human culture. As one zoo admitted in the film *Zoo*,

> You're connecting with another intelligent being who is very happy to participate, be involved. You're not going to be able to ask it about the latest Madonna album; it has no idea what Tolstoy is, or Keats. You can't discuss the difference between Manet and Picasso. That just doesn't exist for their world. It's a simpler, very plain world, and for those few moments you can kind of get disconnected.[84]

Many admit that they regard animals as simply more 'cooperative' or 'convenient' than human partners.[85] They also go to great lengths to 'groom' their animal sexual partners. In the words of an enthusiastic zoophile, adherents would specifically construct barns with padded walls and 'sanitary facilities and cattle breaks, to train the animals in'. Although the main training involved 'kindness and handling', they also engage in 'halter breaking, giving a few titbits, such as sugar', the use of artificial phalluses to accustom the animal to sex with human men and injections of hormones.[86]

Many of the zoos I discuss in this chapter also hold misogynist, even misanthropic, views. Masters sympathetically quotes one zoophile defending his sexual activities on the grounds that 'these animal contacts make men out of boys' and that 'the bestiality spares the community some much worse ills that would have occurred had this barnyard therapy not been available.'[87] In other words, the animal partners were merely things, useful because they prevented a 'natural' impulse for human men to treat women in similar ways. It is not surprising that Masters endorses the view that 'animal contacts' were 'akin to masturbation'.[88] Furthermore, zoos like Matthews write about human females in ways that are so offensive that I refuse to quote them here.[89] He openly admits to his 'hatred of the female half of the human race' and his ingrained distrust of them. Indeed, he sports a tattoo of a topless blonde woman on his belly.[90] Matthews also fails to treat his early sexual experiences with horses in a respectful way. In his words,

> Kinsey said that what he referred to as 'animal contacts' were really just a form of extended masturbation; someone having sex with an animal was just using a living body the way someone else might use a nude photo and some baby oil. I guess that's true of me in a way; after I got my rocks off, I didn't care much what the animal did. I'd just go find a horse when it was convenient, safe, and I was horny enough to make the extra trouble worth it.[91]

The men who gathered at Enumclaw, where Kenneth Pinyan died after being anally penetrated by a stallion, were voracious meat-eaters,[92] suggesting at the very least a cognitive dissonance in their relationship with the animal kingdom more broadly. Others would ensure that they only had sex with animals 'whose early fate at the market was definitively established' – in other words, they targeted animals who were being prepared for slaughter.[93] Many of them focused exclusively on personal interspecies gratification rather than broader questions of politics.

Furthermore, twenty-first-century zoo identities tend to be framed within a conservative discourse of sexuality.[94] Ironically, the movement is often socially traditionalist: monogamy, romantic love and partnerships are highly valued (at least in rhetoric). In the words of Phillip Buble, a zoo who gave evidence before the Maine Criminal Justice Committee in April 2001, he and his dog, Lady, 'live together as a married couple. In the eyes of God, we are truly married.'[95] Other zoos entertain an unrealistic image of an idyllic past – a Garden of Eden – in which humans and animals could live in perfect harmony. This was the image propagated by People United to Restore Eden (PURE), who prefer to be called 'zou' (rather than 'zoo') in order to distance themselves from people they regarded as insufficiently wedded to their vision of sweet concord.[96] The term 'zoophilia' itself suggests that many have not strayed too far from the medicalized model of earlier decades. They are also immersed in a form of sexual identity politics that is more reminiscent of gay movements of the 1970s through to the '90s than of more recent 'queer' framings. What do we find if we move to more queer ways of thinking with sexuality? This is what we turn to in the last chapter.

Five

'Z', or Post-human Love

Define: **Queering.**
Denaturalizing heteronormative categories and practices.

J. R. (Joe) Ackerley was a prominent British author and editor in the first half of the twentieth century. He lived with Queenie, an Alsatian bitch, in a small flat overlooking London's Thames river. Ackerley was madly in love with her. In order to protect her privacy, Ackerley anonymized Queenie's name in his book-long homage to her entitled *My Dog Tulip* (1956). He insisted that the 'only training I ever gave Queenie was to set her free'. After all,

> I did not want a performing dog, I did not want an obedient dog, I did not want a led dog, and I did not want to hurt my dog. I wanted a dog of character, not a slave. I wanted to see Queenie's full personality. Animals have individual characters, like ourselves; I wanted Queenie to develop hers, and character, I believe, can be developed only in an atmosphere of freedom.

He admitted that, when they were apart, he 'sang with joy at the thought of seeing her'.[1]

Their affection was reciprocal. Ackerley recognized Queenie's agency, unhooking that concept from human ideas about will, intentionality and consciousness. He maintained that, on the first day they met, he was conscious of being 'wooed by the most beautiful dog in the world'. It was 'difficult to resist and, like Mignonne the panther in the Balzac story, she had her way in the end'.[2]

For people who did not know her, Queenie was a fairly ordinary-looking dog. Ackerley, however, saw her outer and inner beauty. In two intense pages, he described the contours, colours and textures of Queenie's unique body. 'Her ears are tall and pointed, like the ears of Arubis' (an ancient Egyptian God of the afterlife), he began, adding,

> Her face is long and pointed, basically stone-gray but the snout and lower jaw are jet black. Jet, too, are the rims of her amber eyes, as though heavily mascara'd, and the tiny mobile eyebrow turfs that are set like accents above them . . . Her gray [coat] is the gray of birch bark; her sable tunic is the texture of satin and clasps her long body like a saddle-cloth. No tailor could have shaped it more elegantly.[3]

Most of the rest of the book is concerned with Queenie's unique personality. Some aspects of her temperament exasperated Ackerley, but what could he expect? After all, Queenie possessed a clear sense of her own agency and 'she too has her feelings.'[4] As in all relationships, misunderstandings occurred. Usually, this was Ackerley's fault for failing to listen carefully enough to his partner, even though, by her body language and general comportment, Queenie 'spoke to me as plainly as she could'.[5] Ackerley was also bewildered by the way Queenie's behaviour changed when other people were present. A shrewd veterinary surgeon informed him that 'She's in love with you . . . I expect she's a bit jealous . . . Dogs aren't difficult to understand. One has to put oneself in their position.'[6] Despite occasional squabbles and mix-ups, the relationship between Ackerley and Queenie involved mutual care, respect and sensual enjoyment. Quite simply: they loved each other.

But are ascribing emotions to a dog a form of anthropomorphism? Is 'love' between different species even possible? Crucially: how can we know?

J. R. Ackerley
with Queenie.

This chapter attempts to get to the heart of the debates in this book. Previous chapters explored the changing historical landscape of bestiality and zoophilia, including their theological, psychiatric, philosophical and 'sexual identity' phases. Now, however, I want to set aside questions of harm in order to turn towards issues of pleasure and ethical engagement. Can humans 'love' non-human animals in sensual as well as emotional ways? I seek to address this question in five steps. First, what do we know about the sexual pleasures or libidinal experiences of non-human animals? Second, is it possible to know the intentions, feelings and desires of a non-human animal? Third, can an animal 'consent' to sexual intercourse with a person? Fourth, what about consent to sexual intercourse by other vulnerable subjects, specifically children and people with developmental difficulties? And, fifth, what does it mean to acknowledge the love *for* and *of* animals?

In conclusion, I will be arguing that queer theory can help us understand interspecies erotics. The concept of 'queer' has many meanings. It used to refer to individuals or behaviours designated strange, even weird. From the 1970s onwards, however, the concept was embraced by the gay movement to refer to themselves in positive ways. LGBTQ (lesbian, gay, bisexual, transgender and queer) identities celebrated their difference from heteronormativity. Queer *theorists* have gone even further, deconstructing and rejecting binaries such as heterosexual/homosexual, masculine/feminine, mind/body, reason/emotion, culture/nature and human/animal. They resist the dominant culture's accusation that queer people are unnatural, perverted and offensive. They valorize difference. A queer theorist such as Eve Kosofsky Sedgwick laments the 'cultural practice of sorting people into kinds' and applauds the openness of queer definitions.[7] 'Queer' cross-species love, therefore, can be seen as a further repudiation of attempts to insist on constrained sexualities. But its radical anti-essentialism also sits uneasily with the zoos' demands for rights and their insistence on identity politics. 'Z' or post-human love is the most disruptive of the 'queers'.

Libidinal Experiences of Non-human Animals

What do we know about the sexual pleasure or libidinal experiences of non-human animals? Ackerley had no doubt that Queenie was a desiring subject. Recognizing that 'a full life naturally included the pleasures of sex', Ackerley set about trying to find a 'husband' for Queenie when she came into heat.[8] During this time, he admitted, 'I was touched by the mysterious process and work within her and felt very sweet towards her. She also felt sweet towards me.'[9] He acknowledged that 'I would have been after the pretty creature myself . . . if I had been a dog.'[10]

Clearly, animals have complex sensual lives. Too much of the literature on non-human animals (particularly in the utilitarian tradition) focuses on their vulnerability and pain. But animals also experience pleasure. This is the theme of Jonathan Balcombe's book *Pleasurable Kingdom: Animals and the Nature of Feeling Good* (2006). He points out that all vertebrates have five basic senses and can experience such things as satisfaction, comfort, joy and bliss. While most Western-based scientists who study the sexuality of animals concentrate on matters such as natural selection and reproduction, it is important to observe that animals also *enjoy* sexual play, deliberately seeking it out. In human terms, many animals are 'polysexual'. Both 'wild' and domesticated animals have sexual intercourse with different species to their own.[11] Many relish being caressed and rubbed; they clearly delight in genital-focused games.[12] These games often have nothing to do with procreation. Animals

Jonathan Balcombe giving some much-appreciated attention to Bobby (left) and Parker (right) at the Poplar Spring Animal Sanctuary in Poolesville, Maryland, in March 2012.

masturbate.[13] Female members of certain species have clitorises and engage in genital rubbing and copulation outside of breeding seasons.[14] Some enjoy libidinal encounters with members of their own sex.[15] Many have bodies that are very similar to ours, and while it would be mistaken (as well as anthropomorphic) to ascribe psychic states such as 'desire' to them, it is not unreasonable to assume that they too respond in positive ways to pleasurable and libidinal sensations.

To 'Know' the 'Other'

It is one thing to observe that animals enjoy their own and other bodies, and quite another to ask how people can correctly identify and interpret such feelings. Put another way: can we ever know how another creature (whether human or non-human) feels? The vet's shrewd advice to Ackerley – 'put oneself in their position' – points to this long-standing debate. By their very nature, mental states are subjective; wishes, desires and preferences are 'internal' and invisible. Is the Other always an enigma?

The moral philosopher Adam Smith thought long and hard about these issues. In *The Theory of Moral Sentiments* (1759), Smith admitted that, although people have 'no immediate experience of what other men feel', they could gain an inkling of 'the manner in which they are affected' by 'conceiving what we ourselves should feel in the like situation'. Through acts of imagination, Smith concluded,

> we place ourselves in his situation, we conceive ourselves enduring all the same torments, we enter as it were into his body, and become in some measure the same person with him, and thence form some idea of his sensations, and even feel something which, though weaker in degree, is not altogether unlike them.

In this way, another person's 'agonies' are made manifest, 'and we then tremble and shudder at the thought of what he feels'.[16]

Cynics might respond to Smith's 'theory of moral sentiments' by noting that people usually *fail* to make that empathetic leap into the feelings of others. And most of us will agree that imagination is especially unreliable when the Other does not resemble 'us'. In a witty 1974 article entitled 'What Is It Like to Be a Bat?', the philosopher Thomas Nagel made a pessimistic case for the notion that people are truly capable of putting themselves in an animal's position. To illustrate his arguments, Nagel turned to bats, the second largest order of mammal after rodents. He began by pointing out that bats see the world differently to people. They depend on echolocation (or biological sonar) to detect distance, size, shape, motion and textures. This means that a bat's way of perceiving the world is unlike anything humans can truly conceive of, thus creating 'difficulties for the notion of what it is like to be a bat'. Of course, people can attempt to *imagine* what it would be like to possess bat sensations; we can even try behaving as a bat. But, in reality, this only allows us to imagine 'what it would be like for *me* to behave as a bat behaves'.

Nagel insisted that this should not be used as an excuse for denigrating bat experiences, let alone the complex sociability of their lives. He contended that

> the fact that we cannot expect ever to accommodate in our language a detailed description of . . . bat phenomenology should not lead us to dismiss as meaningless the claim that bats . . . have experiences fully comparable in richness of detail to our own.

Like Smith, Nagel acknowledged the incredible power of imagination. In the final analysis, however,

> this objective ascription of experience is possible only for someone sufficiently similar to the object of ascription to be able to adopt

his point of view . . . The more different from oneself the other experiencer is, the less success one can expect with this enterprise.[17]

While carefully expressed, Nagel's arguments failed to convince everyone. Was it really the case that it is easier to imagine and empathize with the subjective feelings of members of the same species compared with those of other species? What if Nagel's article had been called 'What Is It Like to Be a WASP?': those of us who are not 'White Anglo-Saxon Protestants' might not expect empathy from WASPs, especially male ones. What is really at stake in attempting to 'know' the Other? The philosopher Ralph R. Acampora had another objection to Nagel's arguments. He contended that

There is no need to conduct fanciful thought-experiments or to attempt supernatural exercises in identity-shifting. I do not actually have to become someone else in order to be familiar with that Other.

"I mean, I've got the costume, I've got the gadgets... but I just can't shake the feeling that I'll never know what it's like to be a bat."

Cartoon by Tanya Kostochka in reference to Thomas Nagel's 'What Is It Like to Be a Bat?'

Acampora maintained that it is not necessary 'to know precisely what it is like (hypothetically, in thought) to be that other subject-of-a-life in its own right' since 'it will suffice "merely" to arrive at some sort of comprehension of what it means to be-with other individuals of different yet related species.' In other words, what was required was 'cross-species conviviality'.[18] Perhaps more to the point given the arguments in this book, we are talking about sociability with species such as *Canis familiaris*, with whom we have closely co-evolved since between 9,000 and 30,000 years BCE, not bats.[19]

Creative writers have also critiqued Nagel's position. The best account is that of Nobel laureate J. M. Coetzee. His novel *The Lives of Animals* (1999) features Elizabeth Costello, an Australian novelist and animal lover, who was irritated by Nagel's essay. Costello believed that the 'sensation of being' was a 'heavily affective sensation – of a body with limbs that have extension in space, of being alive to the world'.[20] This was shared by all sentient creatures. She contended that there were 'no bounds to the sympathetic imagination . . . If I can think my way into the existence of a being who never existed, then I can think my way into the existence of a bat or a chimpanzee or an oyster, any being with whom I share the substrate of life.'[21]

Nevertheless, philosophers and novelists do not deny that there are inherent difficulties in 'knowing' what the Other is feeling and desiring. Even Ackerley, with his acute understanding of the desires of Queenie, acknowledged this point. He recalled a night when he was staying with Queenie at a friend's house and Queenie attempted to tell him that she needed to be let out of the room in order to evacuate her bowels. She woke him up, 'rose on her hind legs' and attempted to pull him from his bed; she 'stared intently into my face', then 'hurried over to the door'; she whined, pawed the door and 'snuffled at the bottom of it'. When he ignored her, Queenie found the only place in the room that was not covered with a rug, and . . . 'plop-plop-plop'. Ackerley had not been attentive enough. As he put it,

My pretty animal, my friend, who reposed in me a loving confidence that was absolute, had spoken to me as plainly as she could. She had used every device that lay in her poor brute's power to tell me something, and I had not understood . . . To her it must have seemed that she had been unable to reach me after all. How wonderful to have had an animal come to one to communicate . . . to ask a personal favour! How wretched [for me] to have failed![22]

It is a problem not unique to cross-species communication: human lovers, too, often fail to listen and observe others, even when that lover is speaking 'as plainly as she could'.

Language

One of the chief stumbling blocks in human–animal understanding is the inability of non-human animals to talk in any of the hundreds of human languages (and the inability of humans to speak any one of the millions of animal languages). With the exception of a few primates such as Washoe (the first chimpanzee to be taught human sign language),[23] most animals speak to other members of their species, but not to us. And even if they could talk to us, 'we wouldn't be able to understand', as Ludwig Wittgenstein famously maintained about lions.

We should not, however, conclude that there is therefore little point in speculating about the mental states of other creatures: we can use our senses of sight, smell, sound, taste and touch to understand important aspects of other lives. People do this all the time in human relationships. In fact, a very large proportion of human interactions are non-verbal and, faced with contradictory messages, people tend to believe the non-verbal over the verbal. This is equally true in erotic encounters. A verbal 'yes' or 'no' is not the only – or usual – way to signal consent or non-consent. People routinely guess the wishes of other people through gestures and other signs. Of course, miscommunication is also routine. Most women did not need #MeToo to know that men regularly misread their wishes. There is a better way to put this: men *wilfully* misconstrue sexual desire. In other words, they actually *do* register the meaning behind certain bodily gestures but choose to ignore it.

Furthermore, animals are not the only sentient beings who cannot signal their emotions, desires and preferences through language. A large proportion of us regularly have dealings with vulnerable humans who cannot talk: that is, young infants. Although child abuse is a pervasive problem, most parents do not find it particularly difficult to treat infants according to their capacities. Parents may not know *for certain* what their infant wants, but they are pretty good at inferring her desires from body language and vocalizations.

It is possible, I will be arguing, to extrapolate from the way adult humans communicate with infants to ways we can open up lines of communication between human and non-human animals. A large scientific literature exists that explores parent–child psychology. It shows that it is possible to infer the wishes of preverbal infants by paying careful attention to observable actions and behaviours, including the infant's 'whole-body kinesthetic expressions'.[24]

One example of this expansive field is the work of psychologists Dana Shai and Jay Belsky. In an article entitled 'When Words Just Won't Do' (2011), they introduce a practice called 'parental embodiment mentalizing'. PEM draws on earlier research linking mental states with bodily positions and movements,[25] but applies it to the way parents and other caregivers surmise an infant's underlying mental state. Shai and Belsky place particular emphasis on kinesthetic qualities such as directionality (movements towards or away, for example), tension flow (including the fluidity or rigidity of muscles) and tempo (such as fast and accelerating versus slow and decelerating).[26] They warn against applying PEM in a crude, taxonomical fashion, observing the uniqueness of every relationship and its dyadic nature (in other words, infants as well as their caregivers are engaged in acts of communication). Shai and Belsky are not blasé about PEM. They admit that there is

> an inherent challenge in inferring mental states from observable behavior, so it is often impossible to know what mental state the infant is expressing kinesthetically or what kinesthetic response is more appropriate. In fact, only the infant can judge this.

Nevertheless, they maintain that 'kinesthetic qualities . . . reflect *some* kind of mental state' that a close and careful observer can 'reliably interpret'.[27] They argue that 'embodiment mentalizing' by parents will 'increase the likelihood that individuals will engage in productive, intimate, and sustaining relationships' with nonverbal infants, enabling a feeling of being 'connected to others at a subjective level while maintaining a sense of separateness'.[28] This latter phrase is important: 'embodied mentalizing' does not erase or impose upon the Other but retains knowledge of separate and unique lived-experiences.

'Embodied mentalizing' is a helpful way to think about human/animal communication as well. The affective body enables us to recognize emotions through everyday bodily movements and gestures.[29] People are remarkably good at doing this, even in the absence of verbal cues and facial expressions.[30] Particularly after living together for long periods, companion species clearly make informed guesses about the wishes, desires and preferences of the Other. As with human–infant relationships, by paying attention to the animal's whole-body kinesthetic expressions, people can gain a fairly accurate understanding of the other species, without denying his or her distinctive identity.

This process of interspecies understanding is helped by the large and growing literature illuminating the meanings behind species-specific behaviour. The field of research called 'affective biology' has been particularly informative in rendering more scientific the anecdotal knowledge of animal behaviour often held by animal-lovers. Affective biology takes many forms. Owing to their long and intimate relationships with humans, companion species such as dogs and horses tend to be the most common choices for investigation, although biologists have developed automatic facial recognition of the expressions of other animals, including chimpanzees in the wild.[31] Dogs, though, get the most attention. Researchers have been able to show that dog barks are 'highly variable and differ significantly depending on context and intensity'.[32] For example, a disturbed dog will emit a bark that has 'proportionately more energy at lower frequencies' compared to a dog enjoying play, whose bark has a 'harmoniously rich structure'.[33] Biomedical engineers have devised computer programs that can reliably interpret canine tail language in order to facilitate human–canine interactions.[34] Other scientists have been inspired by research using programs recognizing human speech-patterns to identify emotional states in non-humans. For example, in an article published in the *International Conference on Computing and Informatics* and entitled 'What Is My Dog Trying to Tell Me?', the authors observed the numerous physiological, acoustic and neural similarities between human and mammal vocalizations. They noted that

> All mammals generate their primary acoustic signal at a source, typically rapid pulses of air generated in the lungs, being forced through the vocal folds. The combined action of the vocal tract and the articulators filters their source signal to produce vocalisations. Further, all mammals have similar neurophysiological responses to emotional stimuli, e.g., changes in the brain activity or in the heart rate. Accordingly, changes in the emotional state of an animal should affect the muscular systems used to control the vocal apparatus altering the acoustic properties of the vocalization.[35]

Given these similarities, they used affective computer-based acoustics of dog-barking sequences to analyse the feeling-states of these animals. Their research enabled them to predict not only the context in which the dog was barking, but the nature and intensity of the emotion dogs were experiencing.[36] Indeed, it turns out that it is not strictly necessary to develop computer programs to interpret the language of dog barks and tail waggings at all, since people prove to be quite good at categorizing a dog's feelings through close listening and observation.[37] As everyone from eighteenth-century philosophers to twenty-first-century scientists has predicted, the closer and more regular the engagement between animals and humans, the easier it is to interpret the Other's desires.

Like interactions between adult and infant humans, communication is dialogic. Both humans and animals learn about the Other through meaningful interactions, allowing each to reliably identify emotional states.[38] For example, human body odours produced under emotional conditions were found to 'induce sympathetic and parasympathetic changes' in horses, who responded appropriately.[39] Pet dogs were also able to interpret and respond to emotional states of humans through smelling the chemicals released by people exposed to happy or fearful stimuli.[40] Such interspecies transfers of emotions enabled these animals to predict their owners' needs and preferences.

Neuroimaging has enhanced our understanding. It turns out that dogs can mirror human thoughts and feelings. For example, Gregory Berns trained two dogs to remain still long enough to conduct the first Functional Magnetic Resonance Imaging (fMRI) of a companion species. He not only concluded that dogs might have the same level of consciousness as young children,[41] but found that dogs possessed mirror neurons. In Bern's words,

> In the area just above the caudal there are mirror neurons, the
> kind of neurons that activate our empathetic (involuntary)

copying of another's behavior: you smile and I do likewise. The lighting up of the neurons as well indicates a 'mirroring' of the hand signals of the human that the animal seemed to map onto its paws, the same as when a dog licks its chops when watching humans eat.[42]

The presence of motor neurons suggests that dogs are capable of reading our minds and can be in sympathy with us in deeper ways than have been previously acknowledged.

Of course, the key to interspecies communication is attentiveness. Environmentalist Traci Warkentin had particularly interesting things to say about 'paying attention'. She contended that effective communication

> involves one's whole bodily comportment and a recognition that embodiment is always in relation to social others, both animal and human . . . Embodiment enables the expression of ethical comportment toward others, while also providing a kind of empathic approximation of the experience of others in our midst, which can (and should) inform our responsive interactions with them.[43]

Cultural anthropologist Thomas Csordas and psychologist Kenneth Shapiro have also written extensively about ways of 'attending to and with one's body in surroundings that include the embodied presence of others', as Csordas put it in an important article entitled 'Somatic Modes of Attention' (1997).[44] Csordas insisted on whole-body sensual involvement as a way to understand the meaning behind the embodiments of others. Paying attention to one's own 'bodily dispositions of posture, bearing, and physique' allowed people 'to grasp or recognize' those of other people.[45] Csordas's work was developed in his attempt to understand human practices. In contrast, Kenneth Shapiro's method of 'kinesthetic empathy' directly addressed interspecies interactions, specifically between him and his dog.[46] His technique involved 'an investigatory posture of bodily sensibility adopted to promote empathic access to the meaning implicit in an animal's postures, gestures, and behavior'.[47] In this way, he showed, humans and non-human animals learn to understand each other.

Theoretical approaches to human–animal communication are bolstered by the experiences of people directly involved with animals. The renowned animal scientist Temple Grandin was particularly good at 'reading' the minds of non-human animals, claiming that her autism gave her particular insights into the feelings of animals. 'I place myself inside its body,' she contended, which enabled her to 'imagine what it experiences'.[48] Non-autistic animal-trainers and pet owners also imagined ways to 'put oneself in their position', as Ackerley's vet advised him to do. 'Horse whisperer' Monty Roberts, for example, was able to understand his horses through paying attention to the bodily comportment of his beloved horses, including their stance, eyes, shoulders, head and speed of movement.[49] Still other students of animal behaviour have shown that dogs possess 'partially intentional non-verbal deictic abilities' in order to communicate their desire for (in this example) a favourite toy. Furthermore, the dogs persisted in communicative behaviours even when the human failed to understand their gestures.[50] Indeed, Barbara Smuts maintained that her dog Safi trained *her*.[51] Pet owners routinely discern the preferences, emotional responses and subjectivities of their companion species. People who live with their companion species are fairly accurate in perceiving, sometimes intuitively, what Elizabeth A. Behnke called 'ghost gestures', or micro-movements.[52] These include what a dog is communicating when she points her nose, focuses her gaze, tilts her ears, shifts her weight or jumps to attention. Even the tempo and rhythm of her breathing convey feeling-states. Crucially, these movements do not only reflect species-specific, biological patterns. They are relational and culturally shaped: the dog responds to her owner, learning which movements are most likely to be effective in communication.

Of course, it is important not to overstate the case for human–animal communication. There are insurmountable differences in the ways that humans and animals explore their dyadic relationships. In attempting to divine the Other's wishes, humans prioritize visual senses while dogs are much more olfactory in orientation. This is not surprising since a dog's sense of smell exceeds that of humans about one hundred thousand times.[53] Many errors are made. However, as in the development of human infants, mistakes are part and parcel of the co-creative, emotional process. This was what Dana Shai and Peter Fonagy were arguing when they observed that 'messiness' lies 'at the heart of the development of self and self-regulation' between human adults and infants. They did not think this was wholly negative. After all, 'miscommunication creates negative affect but when interactive errors are repaired, the negative is replaced by positive affect.'[54] Errors could, therefore, result in greater confidence, trust and intimacy. We saw this happening in Ackerley's story about Queenie attempting to tell him about her need to defecate.

It is also not to deny status differentials. Power is never erased in human–animal relationships (or, indeed, any relationship) and just because an animal may have agency, that does not mean that they cannot be exploited. Unlike the abundance of research exploring whole-body kinesthetic expressions between adult and infant humans, there is little interpretative research done on how animal emotions are communicated. Indeed, I could make this point stronger: humans are positively resistant to treating non-human animals as communicable subjects. There is too much cultural, economic and political capital at stake.

Queer Love

For people who love animals and pay careful attention to their needs and preferences, the 'queerness' of animal's libidinal responses can spill into human/non-human relationships. When 'in heat', Ackerley observed in *My Dog Tulip*, Queenie was

> always coming to me as I sat reading or writing, and would push her rump against my knee, gazing at me over her shoulder with an intent look I learnt to know well. She would stay there for a long time, motionless, looking earnestly up at me, until I put down a hand to stroke her head and back, or (which she greatly preferred) her stomach with its little button nipples. Then, as soon as I stopped, she would mount my leg, standing up like a kangaroo to clasp me round the thigh and try to work herself against me.[55]

Ackerley was more honest with his readers in his memoir entitled *My Father and Myself* (1968). There, he confessed that 'In truth, her love and beauty when I kissed her, as I often did, sometimes stirred me physically.' However,

> the thought of attempting to console her myself, even with my fingers, never seriously entered my head. What little I did for her in her burning heat – slightly more than I admitted in *My Dog Tulip* – worried me in my ignorance of animal psychology, in case, by gratifying her clear desires, which were all addressed to me, I might excite and upset her more than she was already excited and upset.

Nevertheless, he acknowledged, he did

> press my hand against the hot swollen vulva she was always pushing at me at these times, taking her liquid upon my palm.

This small easement was, of course, nearer the thing she wanted than to have her back, tail and nipples stroked.[56]

It was a brave admission, and one that dismayed his friends and fans.

In more recent years, though, feminist artists and philosophers have made similar confessions based on their own intimate relations with their companion species. Artists such as Carolee Schneemann have visually represented such forms of interspecies love. In the 1980s and '90s, Schneemann produced a series of photographs entitled *Infinity Kisses*. In them, her cats Cluny and Vesper wake her in the mornings by kissing her lips and mouth. Some of these are extremely erotic: the cats rest on her body, fluids mixing, with their eyes closed in ecstasy.

However, feminist philosophers have been more influential. Most notably, Donna Haraway writes eloquently about her dog, Ms Cayenne Pepper, with whom she engaged in mutual kissing. Echoing Ackerley's overwhelming attraction for Queenie, Haraway claims that Ms Cayenne Pepper's 'darter-tongue kisses have been irresistible . . . Her red merle Australian Shepherd's quick and lithe tongue has swabbed the tissues of my tonsils, with all their eager immune system receptors.' Haraway brazenly admits that

> We have had forbidden conversation; we have had oral intercourse . . . We are, constitutively, companion species . . . Significantly other to each other, in specific difference, we signify in the flesh a nasty developmental infection called love. The love is a historical aberration and a naturalcultural [sic] legacy.[57]

Women's studies scholar Kathy Rudy adds further reflections to those of Haraway. Indeed, she was the thinker who first alerted me to the possibilities of LGBTQ-Z in her landmark 2012 article in *Hypatia: A Journal of Feminist Philosophy*. Rudy uses queer studies to

Carolee Schneemann, *Infinity Kisses*, 1981–7, photographs on linen.

reflect on our relationships (which may or may not include sexual elements) with our dogs. Rudy believes that rights are not the best way to talk about animals. Instead, we should be thinking about affect and advocacy. This would encourage a movement towards affective connections or what she calls the 'change of heart'. She writes:

> I know I love my dogs with all my heart, but I can't figure out
> if that love is sexually motivated . . . What does sex mean? Do
> I think I'm having sex with my dogs when they kiss my face?[58]

Rudy also insists that queering human–animal sexual relations is
not only about human love for animals – but about 'animals loving
us back'.[59] She concludes that the 'sex question' is not particularly
helpful, because what matters is 'recognizing and honoring the
affective bonds many of us share with other creatures'.[60] She believes
that through loving relationships between humans and non-human
animals, *both* partners change: 'The very contours of stable identities
shift under the revolutionary power of love.'[61] It is a reworking of
Donna Haraway's statement in *The Companion Species Manifesto:
Dogs, People, and Significant Otherness* (2003), where she writes
that human–dog relationships are 'co-constitutive . . . none of the
partners preexist the relating, and the relating is never done once
and for all.'[62]

Vulnerability

So far in this chapter, I have argued that animals seek pleasure and
that, through close attentiveness, people can learn to understand
animal preferences, needs and desires. I have also suggested that
all acts of sexual love with animals are not *intrinsically* immoral
or harmful.

But we do have to address the elephant in the room: what about
children? After all, young children can seek sexual love, indicating
by body language and gestures a desire for intimacy. Does that
mean that sex with infants, children and other vulnerable humans
is also legitimate under certain circumstances? This section argues
that human–animal libidinal interactions *cannot* be extrapolated
to acts involving human children. In other words, zoophilia is not
paedophilia.

138

The most flagrant arguments for eradicating the age of consent to sexual intercourse among humans have been made by members of paedophilic communities, most notably the North American Man/Boy Love Association (NAMBLA) and the Paedophile Information Exchange (PIE). It is not my intention to give publicity to their arguments, which I regard as abhorrent. Despite the fact that the age of consent to sexual intercourse has varied widely across time and geographical region (for reasons largely related to ideas about the onset of puberty, different expectations of childhood, shifting views about the innocence or culpability of infants and youth, and the strength of feminist and other activists), these historical and cultural differences cannot be used to justify sex with legally underage children. Just because a child is capable of saying 'yes' to an adult's sexual overtures is no reason to allow it; similarly, even if a child consents in words or with body language, this does not make it acceptable. We forbid sexual relations between adults and children because, although the child might not be able to understand the psychosocial significance of the sexual act in human communities – and, therefore, may even be willing participants – it is likely that, at a later stage, they will understand it. We know that the long-term consequences of that knowledge is invariably traumatic.

This is not the case with non-human animals, who are unlikely to possess the cognitive understanding of the importance of the sex act *for humans*. In other words, human infants and children have the potential to share adult-human understandings of sex in the future and this knowledge is likely to harm them in the future. In contrast, the dog who approaches and voluntarily mounts a human is following his own species-specific 'meaning'. Although we may not know what that 'meaning' actually consists of, our ignorance does not make the dog's actions, and human responses, inherently wrong. There is no reason to insist that animals must possess the *same* understanding about sex as human participants. In other words, it is important not to frame animal sexuality in human terms. What humans think is 'sexual' might not be for the animals involved. They might understand it as being physically groomed (fondling), fed (ingesting ejaculate), relieved (masturbating) or shown affection. Or, indeed, they might barely register the human contact at all.

The situation is different for adults who are categorized as severely intellectually disabled. They are placed by some moral philosophers in a similar moral category to (some) adult animals. Admittedly, making comparisons between intellectually disabled humans and animals is deeply problematic. Although disabled humans are as much 'animals' as their non-disabled counterparts (and therefore none of us should complain about being placed in the same category as other animals), the former are right to be wary of being compared to animals since they have been frequently harmed, even murdered, by processes of dehumanization. The nineteenth-century eugenics movement, early twentieth-century Nazism and late twentieth-century euthanasia debates are obvious examples. Proponents of the Great Ape Project (which include Peter Singer and Paolo Cavalieri) routinely compare severely disabled people with apes, downgrading the former. Philosopher Raymond G. Frey is willing to vivisect human beings whose quality of life is as low as that of certain animals.[63] The sexual lives of non-human animals and intellectually disabled humans have both been stymied by eugenic fears about reproduction: women with developmental difficulties who are sexually active are often portrayed as dangerous vamps and animals who are sexually active with humans also appeared regularly in discussions about freaks and chimeras.

However, some of the insights that advocates for those categorized as profoundly disabled have propounded are useful in helping us understand human–animal relations. Like the scientists and philosophers discussed earlier who explored communicative strategies involving young infants, these activists argue not only that profoundly disabled adults, who are typically non-verbal, *can* communicate their interests and desires, but that non-disabled people have a duty to pay attention to them. Eva Feder Kittay, for example, emphasizes the way carers can recognize the preferences of people with severe intellectual disabilities through 'intimate acquaintance and careful and loving attention'.[64] The most elaborate and convincing of these analyses conceptualize the issue in relation to 'dependent agency'. Philosophers Leslie Pickering Francis and Anita Silvers have written persuasively about the agency of people whose intellectual disabilities mean that they 'cannot independently construct or communicate their own conceptions of the good'.[65] They reject paternalistic or benevolence models involving the imposition of preconceived norms upon people with developmental difficulties, emphasizing instead the need to acknowledge the plurality of preferences and to respect subjective needs. For them, important questions include:

> If others are involved to a significant extent in the formulation of someone's conception of the good, to what extent can that conception be considered that person's own, rather than an objective standard imposed from outside? . . . How can some people assist in formulating their personal ideas of the good without the dependent individual being made vulnerable to exploitation?[66]

Their answer is that independence should not be confused with 'individual scripting'. In other words, the profoundly intellectually disabled person's concept of the 'good' has to always be tailored to reflect that person's 'subjective experiences and personal characteristics', as well as the social contexts (such as those forbidding sex with children) in which all people (disabled or not) live. Respecting the preferences and needs of a person with severe intellectual difficulties is a collaborative process. It requires close and intimate attention being paid to that person's responses, including their bodily movements, vocalizations and other means of expression such as 'ghost gestures'.

Other disability theorists have addressed similar concerns with sexuality explicitly in mind. For example, New York City sex educationalist Fred Kaeser argues for the rights of the intellectually disabled to enjoy sex. He is worried that the same law, regulations and practices that were put in place in order to protect people with learning disorders from sexual harms were excluding them 'from ever engaging in mutual sex behaviors', even when they clearly wanted to do so. He observes that people who have worked with individuals who are severely mentally disadvantaged 'are able to understand fairly well what their likes and dislikes are and whether or not they want certain things'. Relevant questions, he suggests, include

> Do they appear happy and content? Does their body language signal to you that they want to remain involved in the activity? Or, do they appear duressed? Do they try to escape from the activity? Do they seem to be experiencing any discomfort? Have they engaged in the activity willingly? Do they make repeated attempts to engage in the activity on their own?

He promotes what is called the 'smile test', while arguing that it is the duty of carers to 'modify the environment and/or facilitate the individual as the [sexual] activity is engaged in'.[67]

Another revealing analysis of consent and intellectual disability has been made by Deborah W. Denno in an article entitled 'Sexuality, Rape, and Mental Retardation' (1997). She points out that adults with developmental difficulties are 'held to a higher consent standard' than other people, resulting in a situation where 'courts are hurting the very people they are supposed to protect and failing to respect these people's dignity.'[68] Denno suggests that we adopt a 'contextual approach', incorporating what is known about the capacities of intellectually disabled people with an understanding of 'the situational context of the sexual conduct'.[69] If this were to happen, most intellectually disabled adults 'have the capacity to consent to sexual relations, they have the right to do so, and unnecessarily broad and moralistic constructions infringe upon that right'.[70] 'Situational competency' refers to the way an intellectually disabled person 'may be capable of consenting to sexual contact with a certain individual in a particular setting but not to other forms of sexual contact with the same, or other, individuals in other settings'.[71] In this, it is very much like decisions about intimacy made by all of us.

These debates are relevant when we turn to the agency of non-human animals. After all, agency is not an 'all-or-nothing affair'.[72] What is important is the relationship between the different participants and the context in which interactions take place.[73] As with disabled people, assessments need to be made according to knowledge about an individual's capacities and sexual contexts. Legal scholar Antonio Haynes points out that what is behind the prohibition on bestiality is 'the notion that there is something deeply troubling with sexual relationships of unequal power. These relationships are infused with the possibility of coercion.' This is the case in a great many relationships, including 'normal' heterosexual ones, as well as those between agents with very different intellectual capacities. The solution is to develop a 'contextual approach with coercion as a principal feature'.[74] A context-based theory relating to the libidinal conduct of animals might even clarify certain aspects in the ethics of human–human consent. Indeed, it may provide a means by which sexual conduct between humans that is 'legal but seemingly problematic' might be prohibited. Haynes gives the example of a poor woman unable to pay rent:

> If her landlord were to say, 'I will let you miss this month's rent, so long as you have sex with me tonight', many would think that even if the mother agreed to the landlord's demand, something exploitative had occurred. While most modern rape statutes would not read a situation like this, a contextual approach adequately accounting for coercion might.[75]

143

The example also illustrates the difficulties with 'consent' arguments for all sentient creatures, and not just non-human ones.

What the example of adults with developmental difficulties clarifies is the overly restrictive demand for fully informed consent. Very few sexual encounters are in fact 'fully informed' – but that should not automatically mean they are proscribed. Saying 'yes' to someone who has lied about his marital status is different to saying 'yes' to someone who is aware that they are suffering from an active STD. It is the *context* of informed consent that is important. There is no denying that interspecies understanding is particularly challenging, but that is no reason to give up on it altogether, especially when dealing with animals with whom we intimately live.

This is not to deny that the *vast* proportion of human–animal sexual contact is coercive. But it is to suggest that not *all* is, just as the fact that a distressing proportion of acts of sexual intercourse between humans are rape does not mean that sex is rape. The bar must be set very high, however, in order to protect animals and ensure they are not being treated as objects. Human participants must also be given adequate education in the nature of animal experiences.[76] As Margret Grebowicz points out, the 'denaturalizing of animal sexualities' may make it 'impossible to prohibit bestiality preemptively' but it also may make it 'even more urgent' to 'make post-emptive prohibitions upon ethical examination of cultural constructs, beliefs, and practices in the presence of existing power structures'.[77]

This does, however, absolutely *require* a different conception of sexuality – specifically one that is neither phallogocentric or anthropocentric. A phallocentric mode of sexuality, with its emphasis on penetration, force and 'nature', harms animals; an anthropocentric one always confuses them. The most insightful discussion of human–animal libidinal desire can be found in the work of philosopher Monika Bakke. In an essay entitled 'The Predicament of Zoopleasures' (2009), Bakke holds out promise of

144

'Z' (that is, zoopleasures) as disrupting 'the anthropocentric order' by offering an 'alternative to phallocentric models of eroticism'.[78] She maintains that we need a 'postanthropocentric' perspective that pays less attention to 'sexuality understood in terms of instinct and biological compulsion for orgasmic release' and more to forms of sexuality as 'plenitude open to otherness'.[79] This is fundamentally the promise of queerness. Although notoriously fragmented and difficult to pin down, the queer movement is a celebration of formerly transgressive desires. It attempts to push the boundaries of what is 'natural' and 'normal'. By denaturalizing or queering the animal – or, more correctly, companion species – we can take seriously the argument that animals are not simply objects in nature but historical actors in their own right. They are neither symbols nor metaphors. The complexity of their lives is awe-inspiring, as are their sensual needs, desires and preferences. In other words, zoosexuality may offer alternative models of libidinality.

Love

Queenie was Ackerley's intimate companion for more than fifteen years. When she died on 30 October 1961, Ackerley confessed that it was 'the saddest day of my life . . . I shall never stop missing her.' He maintained that 'I would have immolated myself as a suttee when Queenie died . . . For no human would I have done such a thing, but by my love for Queenie I would have been irresistibly compelled.'[80] Ackerley's love was sincere, but it was also precarious owing to societal attitudes towards interspecies love. Prohibitions on sex between human and non-human animals are primarily a function of history – that is, centuries of anxiety and censure. This is a strong reason to move with caution. If bestiality is decriminalized, though, there needs to be a significant tightening of legislation aimed at those who harm animals, as there currently is with regards to the harm of infants, children and 'moral patients'.

145

There is a need, however, to emphasize not only the risks of harm to animals, but their need for affection, companionship and pleasure. Happiness is morally relevant. There are no limits to erotic creativity. We can all imagine ways of being companionate with an animal: a form of trans-species connectedness. Both human and non-human animals experience the world through encounters, collaborations, conflicts and bonds of affection. As I discuss throughout this book, the main ways humans interact with animals – including companion species – are violent, thoughtless and zoocidal. But it doesn't have to be that way. In the words of philosophers Sue Donaldson and Will Kymlicka in *Zoopolis: A Political Theory of Animal Rights*, the first things humans must do is 'recognize that animals are trying to communicate'. We must then be attentive to 'individual repertoires', such as vocalizations and gestures, before 'respond[ing] appropriately'. It is a dialogic, co-created exchange since the animals in our lives must know that 'attempts to communicate with us are not a wasted effort'.[81] As a result, interspecies relationships can be complex, rich and fulfilling. Love – that most intimate and vulnerable emotion – is itself a *coup de foudre*; it is ungovernable. By being 'open to otherness', we might finally find ourselves edging towards becoming true companion species.

References

Introduction

1 Jacques Derrida, 'Force of Law: The "Mystical Foundations of Authority"', trans. Mary Quaintance, *Cardozo Law Review*, 11 (1990), pp. 919–1046 (p. 953).

2 David Levy, *Love + Sex with Robots: The Evolution of Human-robot Relationships* (London, 2008), p. 46.

3 See American Pet Products Association, 'Pet Industry Market Size and Ownership Statistics' (2018), at www.americanpetproducts.org, accessed 30 November 2018.

4 'Estimated Pet Population in the United Kingdom (UK) from 2009 to 2018', in 'Statista', see www.statista.com, accessed 20 January 2018.

5 Jack C. Horn and Jeff Meer, 'The Pleasure of Their Company: PT Survey Report on Pets', *Psychology Today*, XVIII/8 (August 1984), pp. 52–9 (p. 58).

6 For example, see 'Marry Your Pet', at www.marryyourpet.com, accessed 5 March 2019.

7 Marc Shell, 'The Family Pet', *Representations*, 15 (Summer 1986), pp. 121–53. Also see Horn and Meer, 'The Pleasure of Their Company', pp. 52–9, and Jeff Meer, 'Pet Theories: Facts and Figures to Chew On', *Psychology Today*, XVIII/8 (August 1984), pp. 60–67.

8 Immanuel Kant, *Lectures on Ethics*, trans. P. Heath (Cambridge, 1997), p. 156.

9 Peter Morriss, 'Blurred Boundaries', *Inquiry: An Interdisciplinary Journal of Philosophy*, 40 (1997), pp. 259–89 (p. 271).

10 Immanuel Kant, *Groundwork of the Metaphysics of Morals*, trans. and ed. Mary Gregor and Jens Timmerman (Cambridge, 2012).

11 Jacques Derrida, 'The Animal That Therefore I Am (More to Follow)', *Critical Inquiry*, XXVIII/2 (Winter 2002), pp. 369–418 (p. 400).

12 Jason Scott Robert and Françoise Baylis, 'Crossing Species Boundaries', *American Journal of Bioethics*, III/3 (Summer 2003), pp. 1–13 (p. 3).

13 Ibid., p. 4.

14 Adrien Baillet, *La Vie de Monsieur Descartes*, vol. II (Paris, 1691), p. 456.

15 Anil Aggrawal, 'A New Classification of Zoophilia', *Journal of Forensic and Legal Medicine*, 18 (2011), pp. 73–8 (pp. 74–5).

16 Ibid., p. 76.

17 Gary Duffield, Angela Hassiotis and Eileen Vizard, 'Zoophilia in Young Sexual Abusers', *Journal of Forensic Psychiatry*, IX/2 (September 1998), pp. 294–304 (p. 302).

18 Cristina Silva, 'Once Again, Legislature Fails to Outlaw Bestiality', *St Petersburg Times* (6 May 2010), p. 6.

19 A. M. Schenk, C. Cooper-Lehki, C. M. Keelan and W. J. Fremouw, 'Underreporting of Bestiality among Juvenile Sex Offenders: Polygraph versus Self-report', *Journal of Forensic Sciences*, LIX/2 (2014), pp. 540–42.

20 Damian Jacob M. Sendler and Michal Lew-Starowicz, 'Motivation of Sexual Relationship with Animal: Study of a Multinational Group of 345 Zoophiles', *25th European Congress of Psychiatry/European Psychiatry*, 41S [sic] (2017), p. S852.

21 Damian Jacob M. Sendler and Michal Lew-Starowicz, 'Digital Communities of People with Paraphilia: A Study of Zoophiles', *25th European Congress of Psychiatry/European Psychiatry*, 41S [sic] (2017), p. S851.

22 Hani Miletski, 'Zoophilia: Implications for Therapy', *Journal of Sex Education and Therapy*, XXVI/2 (2001), pp. 85–9 (pp. 86–7).

23 For gorillas, see K. A Menninger, 'Totemic Aspects of Contemporary Attitudes towards Animals', in *Psychoanalysis and Culture: Essays in Honor of Géza Róheim*, ed. G. B. Wilbur and W. Muensterberger (New York, 1951), pp. 42–74.

24 Colin J. Williams and Martin S. Weinberg, 'Zoophilia in Men: A Study of Sexual Interest in Animals', *Archives of Sexual Behavior*, XXXII/6 (2003), pp. 523–35. For a detailed exploration of gender preferences, see John C. Navarro and Richard Tweksbury, 'Bestiality: An Overview and Analytic Discussion', *Sociology Compass*, IX/10 (2015), pp. 864–75.

25 Helen M. C. Munro, 'Animal Sexual Abuse: A Veterinary Taboo?', *Veterinary Journal*, CLXXII/2 (2006), pp. 195–7 (pp. 195–6). Also see Helen M. Munro and M. V. Thrusfield, '"Battered Pets": Non-accidental Injuries Found in Dogs and Cats', *Journal of Small Animal Practice*, XLII/6 (June 2001), pp. 279–90; Ranald Munro and Helen M. C. Munro, *Animal Abuse and Unlawful Killing: Forensic Veterinary Pathology* (Edinburgh, 2008), p. 94; Melinda Merck, *Veterinary Forensics: Animal Cruelty Investigations* (Ames, IA, 2007).

26 Alfred C. Kinsey, Wardell B. Pomeroy and Clyde E. Martin, *Sexual Behavior in the Human Male* (Philadelphia, PA, 1948), pp. 670–71 and 675–6.

27 Alfred C. Kinsey, Wardell B. Pomeroy, Clyde E. Martin and Paul H. Gebhard, *Sexual Behavior in the Human Female* (Bloomington, IN, 1953), pp. 502 and 505–6.

28 Morton M. Hunt, *Sexual Behavior in the 1970s* (Chicago, IL, 1974).

29 Marilyn D. Story, 'A Comparison of University Student Experience with Various Sexual Outlets in 1974 and 1980', *Adolescence*, XVII/68 (Winter 1982), pp. 727–47 (p. 742).

30 For example, see William G. Cochran, Frederick Mosteller and John W. Tukey, *Statistical Problems of the Kinsey Report on Sexual Behavior in the Human Male* (Washington, DC, 1954).

31 Stênio de Cássio Zequi, 'The Medical Consequences of Sex between Humans and Animals', in *Sexual Diversity and Sexual Offending: Research, Assessments, and Clinical Treatment in Psychosexual Therapy*, ed. Glyn Hudson Allez (London, 2014), pp. 183–202 (p. 189).

32 Ibid., p. 189.

33 W. Norwood West, 'Sexual Offenders: A British View', *Yale Law Journal*, LV/3 (April 1946), pp. 527–57 (p. 534).

34 For more on the project, see John C. Lilly, *Man and Dolphin* (London, 1962), and John C. Lilly, *Communication between Man and Dolphin: The Possibilities of Talking with Other Species* (New York, 1978).

35 Christopher Riley, 'The Dolphin Who Loved Me: The Nasa-funded Project That Went Wrong', *The Guardian* (8 June 2014), at www.theguardian.com. Also see David Raven, 'Woman Who Had Sex with DOLPHIN during Lab Experiments Speaks Out for the First Time', *Mirror* (9 June 2014), at www.mirror.com.

36 Edgar Gregersen, *Sexual Practices: The Story of Human Sexuality* (London, 1982); Timothy Taylor, *The Prehistory of Sex: Four Million Years of Human Sexual Culture* (London, 1996); Jonas Liliequist, 'Peasants against Nature: Crossing the Boundaries between Man and Animals in Seventeenth and Eighteenth Century Sweden', *Journal of the History of Sexuality*, 1/3 (January 1991), pp. 393–423 (p. 394).

37 Liliequist, 'Peasants against Nature', p. 398.

38 Lucian of Samosata, *True History; and Lucius; or, The Ass*, trans. Paul Turner (London, 1958).

39 Jennifer Milam, 'Rococo Representations of Interspecies Sensuality and the Pursuit of Volupté', *Art Bulletin*, XCVII/2 (2015), pp. 192–209, and Laura Brown, *Homeless Dogs and Melancholy Apes: Humans and Other Animals in the Modern Literary Imagination* (Ithaca, NY, 2010).

40 Alexander Pope, *The Rape of the Lock*, Canto 1, at www.gutenberg.org, accessed 10 June 2019.

41 National Folklore Collection, University College Dublin, vol. DCXXXI, Bantry and Adamstown, Collector Baite Abban (1939), pp. 205–7.

42 'Bamber Gascoigne: A Versatile One-man Band, Getting Faster', *The Times* (6 May 1977), p. 14. For a discussion of the arts and bestiality, see Midas Dekkers, *Dearest Pet: On Bestiality*, trans. Paul Vincent (London, 1994).

43 See also Lenny Bruce's 'Psychopathia Sexualis', at www.youtube.com, accessed 15 March 2019.

44 *Charlotte Rampling: With Compliments* (London, 1987), p. 4.

45 The best discussion can be found in Ted Gott and Kathryn Weir, *Gorilla* (London, 2012).

46 Peter Singer, 'Heavy Petting' (2001), at www.nerve.com.

47 Lee Hall, 'Interwoven Threads: Some Thoughts on Professor Mackinnon's *Of Mice and Men*', *UCLA Women's Law Journal*, XIV/1 (2005), pp. 163–212 (p. 168).

48 Karen Davis, 'Bestiality: Animal Liberation or Human License?', on United Poultry Concerns website (22 April 2001), at www.upc-online.org.

49 Ibid.

50 'Animal Crackers', *Wall Street Journal* (30 March 2001), n.p.

51 Norah Vincent, 'You're an Animal', *Village Voice* (26 March 2001), n.p.

One The Law

1 Doug Brokenshire, *Washington State Place Names from Alki to Yelm* (Caldwell, ID, 1993), p. 70.

2 Rick Anderson, 'Here, Horsey! In 2005, the *Seattle Times*' Report on the Man Who Died', *Seattle Times* (20 April 2010), at www.seattleweekly.com.

3   Charles Mudede, 'Revisiting the Town of the Most Famous Horse Sex Death in Recorded History', *The Stranger* (22 July 2015), at www.thestranger.com.
4   Richard Roesler, 'Senate Bill Would Ban Bestiality', *The Spokesman Review* (13 January 2006), at www.spokesman.com.
5   Ibid.
6   Ibid.
7   Margaret Derry, *Masterminding Nature: The Breeding of Animals, 1750–2010* (Toronto, 2015); Brett Mizett, *Pig* (London, 2011); Kendra Smith-Howard, *Pure and Modern Milk: An Environmental History since 1900* (New York, 2013).
8   Rick Anderson, 'Closing the Barn Door', *Seattle Weekly* (9 November 2005), at www.seattleweekly.com.
9   Washington State Legislature, Section 1 SS8 RCW 16.52.205, at https://apps.leg. wa.gov, accessed 6 January 2019.
10 Wesley J. Smith, 'Horse Sense', *Weekly Standard* (30 August 2005), at www.weeklystandard.com.
11 Doug Clark, 'Bestiality Bill Flimsy Fodder from Capitol', *Spokesman Review* (15 January 2006), at www.spokesman.com.
12 Ibid.
13 For example, see Roesler, 'Senate Bill Would Ban Bestiality', and Mike Baker, 'Bill Banning Bestiality Gets Senate Hearing', *Associated Press State and Local News Wire* (1 February 2006).
14 Anderson, 'Closing the Barn Door'.
15 Nicole Brodeur, 'Bestiality Bill Teaches Lesson in Restraint', *Seattle Times* (2 February 2006), p. B3.
16 'Washington Senate OKs Bestiality Bill', *Spokesman Review* (12 February 2006), at www.spokesman.com.
17 Pam Roach speaking in the film *Zoo*.
18 Editorial Board, 'Bestiality: Yes, It's a Crime', *Seattle Post-Intelligencer* (10 August 2005), p. B6.
19 Wesley J. Smith, 'Horse Sense', *Weekly Standard* (30 August 2005), at www.weeklystandard.com.
20 Ibid.
21 Ibid.
22 'Onwards and Upwards with the Arts', *New Criterion* (February 2007), p. 3.
23 Rob Nelson, 'Interviews: The Dark Horse', *Cinema Scope*, at http://cinema-scope. com, accessed 15 March 2019.
24 Susanna Paasonen, 'The Beast Within: Materiality, Ethics, and Animal Porn', in *Controversial Images*, ed. F. Attwood, V. Campbell, I. Q. Hunter and S. Lockyer (London, 2013), pp. 201–14 (p. 208).
25 Clark, 'Bestiality Bill Flimsy Fodder from Capitol'.
26 Rush Limbaugh in the film *Zoo*.
27 'The Fire Chief and the Sheep', *Smoking Gun* (4 January 2007), at www.thesmokinggun.com, and 'Fire Chief Caught on the Lamb', *Smoking Gun* (7 March 2006), at www.thesmokinggun.com.
28 'Governor Signs Bill to Ban Bestiality', *Tucson Citizen* (24 May 2006).
29 Rebecca F. Wisch, 'Table of State Animal Sexual Assault Law', *Animal Legal and Historical Center* (2016), at www.animallaw.info.
30 'Police Deny Allegation by Shepherd', *The Times* (24 May 1985), p. 2.

31 Joyce E. Salisbury, *The Beast Within: Animals in the Middle Ages* (New York, 1994);
    P. G. Maxwell-Stuart, '"Wild, Filthie, Execrabill, Detestabill, and Unnatural Sin":
    Bestiality in Early Modern Scotland', in *Sodomy in Early Modern Europe*, ed. Tom
    Betteridge (Manchester, 2002), pp. 82–93.

32 Jonas Liliequist, 'Peasants against Nature: Crossing the Boundaries between Man
    and Animals in Seventeenth- and Eighteenth-century Sweden', *Journal of the
    History of Sexuality*, I/3 (January 1991), pp. 393–423 (p. 394).

33 Brian P. Levack, 'The Prosecution of Sexual Crimes in Early Eighteenth Century
    Scotland', *Scottish Historical Review*, LXXXIV/228 (October 2010), pp. 172–93
    (p. 177).

34 Liliequist, 'Peasants against Nature', pp. 393–423 (p. 397).

35 Ibid., p. 401.

36 Doron S. Ben-Atar and Richard D. Brown, *Taming Lust: Crimes against Nature in
    the Early Republic* (Philadelphia, PA, 2014), p. 19.

37 Maxwell-Stuart cited in Courtney Thomas, '"Not Having God before His Eyes":
    Bestiality in Early Modern England', *Seventeenth Century*, XXVI/1 (2011), pp. 149–73
    (p. 155).

38 Erica Fudge, 'Monstrous Acts: Bestiality in Early Modern England', *History Today*,
    L/8 (August 2000), pp. 20–25 (p. 25); Thomas, '"Not Having God before His
    Eyes"', pp. 149–73 (p. 150); John M. Mussin, '"Things Fearful to Name": Bestiality
    in Early America', in *The Animal/Human Boundary: Historical Perspectives*,
    ed. Angela N. H. Creager and William Chester Jordan (New York, 2002),
    pp. 115–56 (p. 116); Liliequist, 'Peasants against Nature', pp. 393–423 (p. 399).

39 Ben-Atar and Brown, *Taming Lust*, p. 19.

40 Ibid.

41 For an example from a French court, see Samantha Hurn, *Humans and Other
    Animals: Cross-cultural Perspectives on Human–Animal Interactions* (London, 2012),
    pp. 1922–93.

42 Ben-Atar and Brown, *Taming Lust*, p. 18.

43 Edward Payson Evans, *The Criminal Prosecution and Capital Punishment of Animals*
    (London, 1906), p. 150.

44 Fabio de Giorgio et al., 'Fatal Blunt Injuries Possibly Resulting from Sexual
    Abuse of a Calf: A Case Study', *Medicine, Science, and Law*, XLIX/4 (2009),
    pp. 307–10 (p. 308). Also see Robert Edward Lee Masters, *Sex-driven People:
    An Autobiographical Approach to the Problem of the Sex-dominated Personality*
    (Los Angeles, CA, 1966), pp. 185–8.

45 Robert Edward Lee Masters, *Forbidden Sexual Behavior and Morality: An Objective
    Re-examination of Perverse Sex Practices in Different Cultures* (New York, 1962),
    pp. 23–4.

46 Roger O. Blevins, 'A Case of Severe Anal Injury in an Adolescent Male Due
    to Bestial Sexual Experimentation', *Journal of Forensic and Legal Medicine*, XVI/7
    (2009), pp. 403–6 (p. 404).

47 Ibid.

48 Ibid.

49 Damian Jacob Sendler, 'Similar Mechanisms of Traumatic Rectal Injuries in
    Patients Who Had Anal Sex with Animals to Those Who Were Butt-fisted by
    Human Sexual Partner', *Journal of Forensic and Legal Medicine*, 51 (2017), pp. 69–73.
    Also see Edoardo Virgilio, Ester Franzese and Salvatore Caterino, 'Zoosexuality:

An Unusual Case of Colorectal Injury', *Acta Chirurgica Belgica*, CXVI/5 (2016), pp. 316–18, and Gueno K. Kirnov, Julian E. Losanoff and Kirren T. Kjossev, 'Zoophilia: A Rare Case of Traumatic Injury to the Rectum', *Injury: International Journal of Care of the Injured*, XXXIII/4 (2002), pp. 367–8.

50 Sdec Zequi, G. C. Guimarães and F. P. da Fonseca, 'Sex with Animals (SWA): Behavioral Characteristics and Possible Association with Penile Cancer. A Multicenter Study', *Journal of Sexual Medicine*, IX/7 (2012), p. 1860.

51 Kelson James Almeida et al., 'Zoophilia and Parkinson's Disease', *Parkinsonism and Related Disorders*, 19 (2013), pp. 1167–8.

52 Stênio de Cássio Zequi, 'The Medical Consequences of Sex between Humans and Animals', in *Sexual Diversity and Sexual Offending: Research, Assessments, and Clinical Treatment in Psychosexual Therapy*, ed. Glyn Hudson Allez (London, 2014), pp. 183–202 (p. 186).

53 Antonio Haynes, 'The Bestiality Proscription: In Search of a Rationale', *Animal Law*, 21 (2014), p. 142.

54 Ibid.

55 *R v. Higson*, 1984, 6 Court of Appeal (England and Wales) p R(S) 20.

56 Home Office, *Setting the Boundaries: Reforming the Law of Sexual Offences* (London, 2000), pp. 126–7.

57 Gabriel Rosenberg, 'How Meat Changed Sex: The Law of Interspecies Intimacy after Industrial Production', *GLQ*, XXIII/4 (2017), pp. 473–506 (p. 481).

58 Jane Cousins, *Make It Happy: What Sex Is All About* (London, 1978), p. 103, and Jane Cousins, *Make It Happy: What Sex Is All About* (Harmondsworth, 1986), p. 123.

59 'MP Supports Parents over Sex Education', *The Times* (9 February 1980), p. 3. Jane Cousins-Mills published an article about this book entitled '"Putting Ideas into Their Heads": Advising the Young', *Feminist Review*, 28 (January 1988), pp. 163–74, but does not mention the controversy over bestiality. Rather, she emphasizes the unease about mentioning child sexual abuse and incest.

60 Jane Cousins-Mills, *Make It Happy, Make It Safe: What Sex Is All About* (London, 1988).

61 Diane Richard, 'Forbidden Love', *Contemporary Sexuality: An International Resource for Educators, Researchers, and Therapists*, XXXV/10 (October 2001), pp. 1, 4–7 (p. 6).

62 Richard, 'Forbidden Love', pp. 1, 4–7 (p. 5).

63 Luke Johnson, 'Rick Santorum Defends Interview Linking Homosexuality to "Man on Dog" Sex', *Huffington Post* (1 May 2012).

64 Ralph McInerny, 'Animal Husbandry', *Catholic Thing* (3 September 2008), at www.thecatholicthing.org, accessed 28 March 2019.

65 Richard, 'Forbidden Love', pp. 1, 4–7 (p. 5).

66 'No Sex with Animals: Ohio Enacts Bestiality Law', *Spokesman Review* (27 March 2017), at www.spokesman.com, accessed 5 January 2019.

67 Cited in Rebecca Cassidy, 'Zoosex and Other Relationships with Animals', in *Transgressive Sex: Subversion and Control in Erotic Encounters*, ed. Hastings Donnan and Fiona Magowan (Oxford, 2009), pp. 91–112 (p. 105).

68 Richard, 'Forbidden Love', pp. 1, 4–7 (p. 7).

69 Ibid.

70 Rosenberg, 'How Meat Changed Sex', p. 481.

71 For a discussion, see Emily Malhiot, 'Chapter 86: Nevada Finally Outlaws Bestiality', *University of the Pacific Law Review*, 49 (2017), pp. 473–506 (p. 569).

72 Rebekah Ranger and Paul Federoff, 'Commentary: Zoophilia and the Law', *Journal of the American Academy of Psychiatry and the Law*, XLII/4 (2014), pp. 421–6 (p. 423). See Rhode Isl. Stat. Ann. § 11–10–1 (1938), and RI Gen. Laws § 11–37–8.1, 11–37–8.3, 11–37–6 (2014).

73 For a discussion, see Michael Roberts, 'The Unjustified Prohibition against Bestiality: Why the Laws in Opposition Can Find No Support in the Harm Principle', *Journal of Animal and Environmental Law*, 1 (2009–10), pp. 176–221 (pp. 184–91). For a detailed analysis, state by state, see Gieri Bolliger and Antoine F. Goetschel, 'Sexual Relations with Animals (Zoophilia): An Unrecognized Problem in Animal Welfare Legislation', in *Bestiality and Zoophilia: Sexual Relations with Animals*, ed. Andrea M. Beetz and Anthony L. Podberscek (West Lafayette, FL, 2005), pp. 23–45 (pp. 34–5).

74 *Murray v. State of Indiana*, 143 NE 2d 290, in Justia U.S. Law, at http://law.justia. com, accessed 9 February 2019.

75 *State v. Bonynge*, 450 NW 2d. 331 (Minnesota Court of Appeal, 1990), in Justia U.S. Law, at http://law.justia.com, accessed 9 February 2019.

76 For example, see *People v. Carrier*, 254 NW 2d. 35 (Michigan Court of Appeal, 1977), in Court Listener, at www.courtlistener.com, accessed 9 February 2019.

77 *Murray v. State of Indiana*, 143 NE 2d 290, in Justia U.S. Law, at http://law.justia. com, accessed 9 February 2019.

78 Jim Schaefer, 'Sheep Abuser Is Center of Debate: Man Fights Inclusion on Sex Offender Registry', *Detroit Free Press*, B1 (3 March 2006), at www.ar15.com.

79 Sexual Offences Act 2003, s.69, at www.legislation.gov.uk, accessed 6 January 2019.

80 Kevin J. Stafford and David J. Mellor, 'Painful Husbandry Procedures in Livestock and Poultry', in *Improving Animal Welfare: A Practical Approach*, ed. Temple Grandin (Wallingford, Oxfordshire, 2010), pp. 88–113.

81 Ibid., pp. 88–113.

82 'Arizona Revised Statute 13, Criminal Code, 13–1411-C. Bestiality; Classification; Definition', at https://codes.findlaw.com/az, accessed 2 February 2019.

83 '8-step Guide to Artificially Inseminating a Dairy Cow', *Farmers Weekly* (5 November 2015), at www.fwi.co.uk.

84 Matthew Shea, 'Punishing Animal Rights Activists for Animal Abuse: Rapid Reporting and the New Wave of AgGag Laws', *Columbia Journal of Law and Social Problems*, XLVIII/3 (2015), pp. 337–8.

85 Karen Davis, *The Holocaust and the Henmaid's Tale: A Case for Comparing Atrocities* (New York, 2005), p. xiv.

86 Karen Davis, 'Bestiality: Animal Liberation or Human License?' (22 April 2001), at www.upc-online.org.

Two Cruelty to Animals

1 Catharine A. MacKinnon, 'Of Mice and Men: A Feminist Fragment on Animal Rights', in *Animal Rights: Current Debates and New Directions*, ed. Cass R. Sunstein and Martha Craven Nussbaum (Oxford, 2004), pp. 263–76 (p. 267).

2 Linda Lovelace with Mike McGrady, *Ordeal* [1980] (London, 1981), p. 92.

3 Ibid.

4 Marty Rimm, 'Marketing Pornography on the Information Superhighway: A Survey of 917,410 Images, Descriptions, Short Stories, and Animations

Downloaded 8.5 Million Times by Consumers in over 2,000 Cities in Forty Countries, Provinces, and Territories', *Georgetown Law Journal*, 83 (1994–5), pp. 1849–934. Also see Robert E. Jenkins and Alexander R. Thomas, *Deviance Online: Portrayals of Bestiality on the Internet* (New York, 2004), p. 12.

5 Lovelace with McGrady, *Ordeal*, pp. 91–2.

6 Ibid., p. 157.

7 Ibid., pp. 76–7.

8 Ibid., pp. 143–4.

9 Ibid., pp. 35–6.

10 Ibid., p. 94.

11 René Descartes, *Discourse on Method and Other Writings*, ed. F. E. Sutcliffe (Harmondsworth, 1968), pp. 73–6.

12 I discuss this at length in *What It Means to Be Human: Historical Reflections from 1791 to the Present* (London, 2011).

13 Peter Harrison, 'Do Animals Feel Pain?', *Philosophy*, LXVI/255 (January 1991), pp. 25–40. For a spirited refutation of Harrison's arguments, see Ian House, 'Harrison on Animal Pain', *Philosophy*, LXVI/257 (July 1991), pp. 376–9.

14 J. R. Ackerley, *My Dog Tulip* [1956] (New York, 1999), p. 95.

15 Helen M. C. Munro and M. V. Thrusfield, 'Battered Pets: Sexual Abuse', in *Bestiality and Zoophilia: Sexual Relations with Animals*, ed. Andrea M. Beetz and Anthony L. Podberscek (West Lafayette, IN, 2005), p. 71. Also see Helen M. C. Munro and M. V. Thrusfield, 'Battered Pets: Non-accidental Injuries Found in Dogs and Cats', *Journal of Small Animal Practice*, XLII/6 (2001), pp. 279–90, and Anton Hvozdík et al., 'Ethological, Psychological, and Legal Aspects of Animal Sexual Abuse', *Veterinary Journal*, CLXXII/2 (2006), pp. 374–6.

16 Gieri Bolliger and Antoine F. Goetschel, 'Sexual Relations with Animals (Zoophilia): An Unrecognized Problem in Animal Welfare Legislation', in *Bestiality and Zoophilia*, ed. Beetz and Podberscek, pp. 23–45 (p. 36).

17 Damian Jacob M. Sendler and Michal Lew-Starowicz, 'Rethinking Classification of Zoophilia', *25th European Congress of Psychiatry/European Psychiatry*, 41S (2017), p. S851. Also see Wilhelm Stekel, *Patterns of Psychosexual Infantilism*, ed. Emil A. Gutheil (New York, 1952), pp. 265–6.

18 Andrea M. Beetz, 'Bestiality/Zoophilia: A Scarcely Investigated Phenomenon between Crime, Paraphilia, and Love', *Journal of Forensic Psychology Practice*, IV/2 (2004), pp. 1–36 (p. 14).

19 Erika Cudworth, '"Most Farmers Prefer Blondes": Social Intersectionality and Species Relations', in *Humans and Other Animals*, ed. B. Carter and N. Charles (London, 2011), pp. 153–72 (pp. 168–9).

20 For example, see Shawna Flavell, 'Sexual Abuse of Animals: A Recurring Theme on Factory Farms', PETA website (13 September 2010), at www.peta.org: it includes an extremely graphic video. Also see Shawna Flavell, 'Four More Former Iowa Pig Factory Farm Workers Admit Guilty', PETA website (24 June 2009), at www.peta.org.

21 Peter Moskowitz, 'Idaho Gov. Signs "Ag Gag" Bill into Law', *Al Jazeera America* (2014), at http://america.aljazeera.com, accessed 15 March 2019.

22 Mark Matthews, *The Horse-man: Obsessions of a Zoophile* (New York, 1994), p. 51. Also see p. 159.

23 Bolliger and Goetschel, 'Sexual Relations with Animals (Zoophilia)', pp. 23–45 (p. 39).

24 Hvozdík et al., 'Ethological, Psychological, and Legal Aspects of Animal Sexual Abuse', pp. 374–6 (p. 375), and Helen M. C. Munro, 'Animal Sexual Abuse', *Veterinary Journal*, CLXXII/2 (2006), pp. 195–7 (p. 195). For comparisons with the grooming of children, see G. Duffield, A. Hassiotis and E. Vizard, 'Zoophilia in Young Sexual Abusers', *Journal of Forensic Psychiatry*, 9 (1998), pp. 294–304, and Christopher J. Hobbs, Helga G. I. Hanks and Jane M. Wynne, 'Sexual Abuse: The Scope of the Problem', in *Child Abuse and Neglect: A Clinician's Handbook*, 2nd edn, ed. Hobbs, Hanks and Wynne (London, 1999), pp. 165–89.

25 Tom Regan, *The Case for Animal Rights* (London, 1983), pp. 327–9.

26 Bolliger and Goetschel, 'Sexual Relations with Animals (Zoophilia)', pp. 23–45 (pp. 38–9 and 42).

27 Piers Beirne, 'Rethinking Bestiality: Towards a Concept of Interspecies Sexual Assault', *Theoretical Criminology*, 1/3 (1997), pp. 317 and 326. Also see Piers Beirne, 'Rethinking Bestiality: Towards a Concept of Interspecies Sexual Assault', in *Companion Animals and Us: Exploring the Relationships between People and Pets*, ed. Anthony L. Podberscek, Elizabeth S. Paul and James A. Serpell (Cambridge, 2000), pp. 313–31.

28 Piers Beirne, 'On the Sexual Assault of Animals: A Sociological View', in *The Human/Animal Boundary: Historical Perspectives*, ed. Angela N. H. Creager and William Chester Jordon (New York, 2002), pp. 193–227 (p. 203).

29 Ibid., p. 203.

30 Beirne, 'Rethinking Bestiality', pp. 313–31 (p. 327). Also see Carol J. Adams, 'Woman-battering and Harm to Animals', in *Animals and Women: Feminist Theoretical Explorations*, ed. Adams and Josephine Donovan (Durham, 1995), pp. 55–84.

31 Bourke, *What It Means to Be Human*.

32 Melinda Merck, *Veterinary Forensics: Animal Cruelty Investigations* (Ames, IA, 2007), pp. 225–32.

33 Ranald Munro and Helen M. C. Munro, *Animal Abuse and Unlawful Killing: Forensic Veterinary Pathology* (Edinburgh, 2008), p. 94. Also see Leslie Sinclair, Melinda Merck and Randall Lockwood, *Forensic Investigation of Animal Cruelty: A Guide for Veterinary and Law Enforcement Professionals* (Washington, DC, 2006), pp. 173–8.

34 Phyllis DeGioia, 'Recognizing Sexual Abuse in Animals', in Vin News Service (5 March 2015), in news.vin.com.

35 I. Imbschweiler et al., 'Animal Sexual Abuse in a Female Sheep', *Veterinary Journal*, CLXXXII/3 (2009), pp. 481–3 (p. 481).

36 Munro, 'Animal Sexual Abuse', pp. 195–7 (p. 196). Also see Melinda Merck, *Veterinary Forensics: Animal Cruelty Investigations* (Ames, IA, 2007), p. 225.

37 Stacy A. Nowicki, 'On the Lamb: Toward a National Animal Abusers Registry', *Animal Law*, 17 (2010), pp. 197–242.

38 Emily Malhiot, 'Chapter 86: Nevada Finally Outlaws Bestiality', *University of the Pacific Law Review*, 49 (2017), pp. 556–73 (p. 562).

39 Robert E. Jenkins and Alexander R. Thomas, *Deviance Online: Portrayals of Bestiality on the Internet* (New York, 2004), pp. 8 and 12.

40 For a discussion, see Margret Grebowicz, 'When Species Meat: Confronting Bestiality Pornography', *Humanimalia*, 1/2 (Spring 2010), at www.depauw.edu.

41 Randy Malamud, *An Introduction to Animals and Visual Culture* (Basingstoke, 2012), pp. 105–9.

42 Ibid., p. 94.

43 Jack Stevenson, 'Dead Famous: The Life and Movies of Erotic Cinema's Most Exploited Figure, Bodil Joensen', in *Fleshpot: Cinema's Sexual Myth Makers and Taboo Breakers,*
ed. Stevenson (Manchester, 2000), p. 180.

44 See the 2006 British documentary *The Dark Side of Porn: The Real Animal Farm.*

45 Statement by Nancy Perry, the Vice President for Government Affairs in the Humane Society of the United States, in *Prohibiting Obscene Animal Crush Videos in the Wake of United States v. Stevens. Hearing before the Committee on the Judiciary United States Senate One Hundred Eleventh Congress. Second Session. September 15, 2010. Serial No. J–111–108* (Washington, DC, 2011), p. 3.

46 Statement by U.S. Senator Dianne Feinstein, ibid., p. 32.

47 Statement by Nancy Perry, p. 3.

48 Aelian, *On the Characteristics of Animals*, trans A. F. Schofield, I.1 and XVI.3 (Cambridge, MA, 1958), pp. 21 and 305.

49 Samuel Pepys, *The Diary of Samual Pepys* [1661] (Coln St Aldwyns, 2006), p. 90.

50 National Folklore Collection, University College Dublin, vol. MCCCLXXXIX (1955), p. 180, Collector Michael J. Murphy, relating to Glenariffe (County Antrim).

51 Orson Squire Fowler, *Creative and Sexual Science; or, Manhood, Womanhood, and Their Mutual Relations* (London, 1904), p. 676.

52 Robert Edward Lee Masters, *Sex-driven People: An Autobiographical Approach to the Problem of the Sex-dominated Personality* (Los Angeles, CA, 1966), p. 155.

53 Ibid., p. 155.

54 Ibid., p. 156.

55 Edward Long, *The History of Jamaica; or, General Survey of the Antient and Modern State of That Island with reflections on its Situation, Settlements, Inhabitants, Climate, Products, Commerce, Laws, and Government*, vol. II (London, 1774), pp. 360 and 364–5.

56 Dr Thomas Stewart Traill, 'Observations on the Anatomy of the Orang Outang', *Memoirs of the Wernerian Natural History Society*, 3 (1821), n.p., paper was read on 7 February 1818.

57 Sir Richard Francis Burton, 'Foreword', in Count Roscaud, *Human Gorillas: A Study of Rape with Violence* (Paris, 1901), pp. i–viii (p. viii).

58 Ibid., p. viii.

59 Roscaud, *Human Gorillas*, p. 9.

60 Ibid. Note that I have silently corrected a typo: 'with' was spelt 'nith'.

61 Ibid., p. 14.

62 Ibid., p. 15.

63 Ibid.

64 Ibid.

65 Ibid., p. 17.

66 Ibid.

67 Ibid.

68 Ibid., p. 19.

69 Ibid.

70 Ibid., p. 20.

71 Ibid., p. 2.
72 Ibid.
73 Ibid., p. 4.

Three Mad or Bad?

1 Richard von Krafft-Ebing, *Psychopathia Sexualis: A Medico-forensic Study* [1886] (London, 1939), pp. 532–4 and 561–2.

2 Sigmund Freud, *Three Essays on the Theory of Sexuality*, trans. James Strachey (London, 1949), p. 27. Freud did not believe that bestialists were necessarily insane.

3 Léon-Henri Thoinot, *Medicolegal Aspects of Moral Offenses*, trans. Arthur Wisswold Weysse (Philadelphia, PA, 1911), p. 444. It was originally published as *Attentats aux moeurs et perversions du sens genital* (Paris, 1898).

4 Ibid., p. 444.

5 Thoinot, *Medicolegal Aspects of Moral Offenses*, p. 445.

6 Ibid.

7 Ibid., p. 446.

8 Ibid.

9 Gaston Dubois-Desaulle, *Bestiality: An Historical, Medical, Legal, and Literary Study*, translated from the French with addenda by 'A.F.N.' (New York, 1933), pp. 120 and 142. Its French title was *Étude sur la bestialité au point de vue historique, médical et juridique* (Paris, 1905).

10 Samuel H. Ruskin, 'Analysis of Sex Offenses among Male Psychiatric Patients', *American Journal of Psychiatry*, XCVII/4 (January 1941), pp. 955–68 (p. 964). This point was also made by Vinka Lesandrić et al., 'Zoophilia as an Early Sign of Psychosis', *Alcoholism and Psychiatry Research*, 53 (2017) pp. 27–32.

11 Manjeet Singh Bhatia, Shruti Srivastava and Sumeet Sharma, 'An Uncommon Case of Zoophilia: A Case Report', *Medicine, Science, and the Law*, XLV/2 (2005), pp. 174–5; Edward Allen Clifford, *The Sexual Perversions and Abnormalities*, 2nd edn (London, 1949), p. 326; L. Shenken, 'Psychotherapy in a Case of Bestiality', *American Journal of Psychotherapy*, 14 (1960), pp. 728–40; W. Norwood East, 'Sexual Offenders: A British View', *Yale Law Journal*, LV/3 (April 1946), pp. 527–57 (p. 534); Daniel T. Wilcox, Caroline M. Foss and Margerite L. Donathy, 'Working with Zoosexual Offenders (Addressing High Levels of Deviance)', in *Sex Offender Treatment: A Case Study Approach to Issues and Interventions*, ed. Wilcox, Tanya Garrett and Leigh Harkins (Chichester, 2015), pp. 242–66 (pp. 243–4).

12 Commented on in Manuel F. Casanova, Glenn Mannheim and Markus Kruesi, 'Hippocampal Pathology in Two Mentally Ill Paraphilics', *Psychiatric Research Neuroimaging*, CXV/1–2 (2002), pp. 79–89 (p. 79).

13 Robert Edward Lee Masters, *Forbidden Sexual Behavior and Morality: An Objective Re-examination of Perverse Sex Practices in Different Cultures* (New York, 1962), p. 120; M. Dekkers, *Dearest Pet: On Bestiality* (New York, 1994); R.E.L. Masters, *Sex-driven People: An Autobiographical Approach to the Problem of the Sex-dominated Personality* (Los Angeles, CA, 1966); Allen Edwardes and R.E.L. Masters, *The Cradle of Erotica: A Study of Afro-Asian Sexual Expression and an Analysis of Erotic Freedom in Social Relationships* (New York, 1963), p. 242; B. Sardar Singh, *A Manual of Medical Jurisprudence for Police Officers* (Moradabad, 1916), pp. 76–7; M. Dekkers, *Dearest Pet:*

On Bestiality (New York, 1994); Edwardes and Masters, *The Cradle of Erotica*, p. 243; Edgar Gregersen, *Sexual Practices: The Story of Human Sexuality* (London, 1982); John Money, *Lovemap: Clinical Concepts of Sexual/Erotic Health and Pathology, Paraphilia, and Gender Transposition in Childhood, Adolescence, and Maturity* (New York, 1986).

14 Krafft-Ebing, *Psychopathia Sexualis*, p. 561.

15 Philip Q. Roche, 'Sexual Deviations', *Federal Probation*, 14 (1950), pp. 3–11 (p. 9).

16 I. D. Craig, 'Bestiality', *Police Surgeon: Journal of the Association of Police Surgeons of Great Britain*, 20 (November 1981), pp. 41–4 (p. 42). Also see Andrea M. Beetz, 'Bestiality/Zoophilia: A Scarcely Investigated Phenomenon between Crime, Paraphilia, and Love', *Journal of Forensic Psychology Practice*, IV/2 (2004), pp. 1–36 (p. 17); Gerald H. Cerrone, 'Zoophilia in a Rural Population: Two Case Studies', *Journal of Rural Community Psychology*, XII/1 (Summer 1991), pp. 29–39; Sigmund Freud, *Three Essays on the Theory of Sexuality*, authorized translation by James Strachey (London, 1949), p. 27; Masters, *Forbidden Sexual Behavior and Morality*, p. 45; Daniel T. Wilcox, Caroline M. Foss and Margerite L. Donathy, 'A Case Study of a Male Sex Offender with Zoosexual Interests and Behaviors', *Journal of Sexual Aggression*, XI/3 (September 2005), pp. 305–17.

17 Craig, 'Bestiality', pp. 41–4 (p. 42).

18 Ibid.

19 American Psychiatric Association, *Diagnostic and Statistical Manual: Mental Disorders* (Washington, DC, 1952), p. 39.

20 American Psychiatric Association, *Diagnostic and Statistical Manual of Mental Disorders*, 3rd edn (Washington, DC, 1980), p. 270.

21 American Psychiatric Association, *Diagnostic and Statistical Manual of Mental Disorders*, revd 3rd edn (Washington, DC, 1987), p. 270; Gene G. Abel et al., 'Multiple Paraphilic Diagnoses among Sex Offenders', *Bulletin of the American Academy of Psychiatry and Law*, VI/2 (1988), pp. 153–68.

22 American Psychiatric Association, *Diagnostic and Statistical Manual of Mental Disorders*, 4th edn (Washington, DC, 1994), p. 523.

23 Rebekah Ranger and Paul Federoff, 'Commentary: Zoophilia and the Law', *Journal of the American Academy of Psychiatry and the Law*, XLII/4 (2014), pp. 421–6 (p. 422).

24 Masters, *Forbidden Sexual Behavior and Morality*, pp. 4, 124 and 44. Emphasis added.

25 Ibid., pp. 120–21. Masters also makes this point in *Sex-driven People*, p. 124.

26 Masters, *Forbidden Sexual Behavior and Morality*, pp. 81–2.

27 William A. Alvarez and Jack P. Freinhar, 'A Prevalence Study of Bestiality (Zoophilia) in Psychiatric In-patients, Medical In-patients, and Psychiatric Staff', *International Journal of Psychosomatics*, XXXVIII/1 (1991), pp. 45–7.

28 G. A. Hassiotis Duffield and E. Vizard, 'Zoophilia in Young Sexual Abusers', *Journal of Forensic Psychiatry*, IX/2 (1998), pp. 294–304 (p. 301).

29 William M. Fleming, Brian Jory and David L. Burton, 'Characteristics of Juvenile Offenders Admitting to Sexual Activity with Nonhuman Animals', *Society and Animals*, X/1 (2002), pp. 31–45.

30 Gene G. Abel et al. (1987), cited in Daniel T. Wilcox, Caroline M. Foss and Margerite L. Donathy, 'A Case Study of a Male Sex Offender with Zoosexual Interests and Behaviors', *Journal of Sexual Aggression*, XI/3 (September 2005), pp. 305–17; Gene G. Abel and Joanne L. Rouleau, 'The Nature and Extent of Sexual Assault', in *Handbook of Sexual Assault*, ed. W. L. Marshall, D. R. Laws and H. G. Barbaree (New York, 1990), pp. 9–21.

31 Rebecca L. Bucchieri, 'Bridging the Gap: The Connection between Violence against Animals and Violence against Humans', *Journal of Animal and Natural Resource Law*, 11 (2005), pp. 115–35 (p. 123).

32 Gary Duffield, Angela Hassiotis and Eileen Vizard, 'Zoophilia in Young Sexual Abusers', *Journal of Forensic Psychiatry*, IX/2 (September 1998), pp. 294–304 (p. 301).

33 Alvarez and Freinhar, 'A Prevalence Study of Bestiality (Zoophilia) in Psychiatric In-patients, Medical In-patients, and Psychiatric Staff', pp. 45–7 (p. 45).

34 Karla S. Miller and John F. Knutson, 'Reports of Severe Physical Punishment and Exposure to Animal Cruelty by Inmates Convicted of Felonies and by University Students', *Child Abuse and Neglect*, XXI/1 (1997), pp. 59–82.

35 Christopher Hensley and Suzanne E. Tallichet, 'Animal Cruelty Motivations: Assessing Demographic and Situational Factors on Animal Cruelty Motivations', *Journal of Interpersonal Violence*, XX/11 (2005), pp. 1429–43.

36 Christopher Hensley, Suzanne E. Tallichet and S. D. Singer, 'Exploring the Possible Link between Childhood and Adolescent Bestiality and Interpersonal Violence', *Journal of Interpersonal Violence*, XXI/7 (2006), pp. 910–23, and Christopher Hensley, Suzanne E. Tallichet and Erik L. Dutkiewicz, 'Examining Demographic and Situational Factors on Animal Cruelty Motivations', *International Journal of Offender Therapy and Comparative Criminology*, LV/3 (2010), pp. 492–502.

37 Christopher Hensley, Suzanne E. Tallichet and Erik L. Dutkiewicz, 'The Predictive Value of Childhood Animal Cruelty Methods on Later Adult Violence: Examining Demographic and Situational Correlates', *International Journal of Offender Therapy and Comparative Criminology*, LVI/2 (2012), pp. 281–95 (pp. 281 and 292).

38 Daniel T. Wilcox, Caroline M. Foss and Marguerite L. Donathy, 'A Case Study of a Male Sex Offender with Zoosexual Interests and Behaviors', *Journal of Sexual Aggression*, XI/3 (September 2005), pp. 305–17. Arguments that bestialists would go on to harm humans are common in the literature. For example, see F. R. Ascione, 'The Abuse of Animals and Human Interpersonal Violence', in *Child Abuse, Domestic Violence, and Animal Abuse*, ed. Ascione and P. Arkow (West Lafayette, IN, 1999), pp. 50–61; F. R. Ascione, 'Children Who Are Cruel to Animals: A Review of Research and Implications for Developmental Psychopathology', in *Cruelty to Animals and Interpersonal Violence*, ed. L. Lockwood and Ascione (West Lafayette, IN, 1998), pp. 83–104; Gary Duffield, Angela Hassiotis and Eileen Vizard, 'Zoophilia in Young Sexual Abusers', *Journal of Forensic Psychiatry*, IX/2 (September 1998), pp. 294–304.

39 Andrea M. Beetz, 'Bestiality/Zoophilia: A Scarcely Investigated Phenomenon between Crime, Paraphilia, and Love', *Journal of Forensic Psychology Practice*, IV/2 (2004), pp. 1–36 (p. 26).

40 Lacey Levitt, Tia A. Hoffer and Ann B. Loper, 'Criminal Histories of a Subsample of Animal Cruelty Offenders', *Aggression and Violent Behavior*, 30 (2016), pp. 45–58 (p. 50).

41 Ibid., pp. 45–58 (p. 50).

42 Ibid.

43 Manuel F. Casanova, Glenn Mannheim and Markus Kruesi, 'Hippocampal Pathology in Two Mentally Ill Paraphilics', *Psychiatry Research: Neuroimaging*, 115 (2002), pp. 79–89 (p. 84).

44 Richard J. McNally and Brian M. Lukach, 'Behavioral Treatment of Zoophilic Exhibitionism', *Journal of Behavioral Therapy and Experimental Psychology*, XXII/4 (1991), pp. 281–4 (p. 282).

45 Ibid.

46 Ibid.

47 Ibid., pp. 281–4 (p. 283).

48 Ibid.

49 For examples, see Gerald H. Cerrone, 'Zoophilia in a Rural Population: Two Case Studies', *Journal of Rural Community Psychology*, XII/1 (Summer 1991), pp. 29–39, and Wilcox, Foss and Donathy, 'A Case Study of a Male Sex Offender with Zoosexual Interests and Behaviors', pp. 305–17.

50 For example, see Ruskin, 'Analysis of Sex Offenses among Male Psychiatric Patients', pp. 955–68 (p. 964).

51 Rebekah Ranger and Paul Federoff, 'Commentary: Zoophilia and the Law', *Journal of the American Academy of Psychiatry and the Law*, XLII/4 (2014), pp. 421–6 (p. 422).

52 Ibid., pp. 421–6 (p. 425).

53 Allen Frances, 'DSM5 and Sexual Disorders; Just Say No', *Psychiatric Times* (18 March 2010), n.p.

54 Allen Frances, 'The Latest in Sexually Violent Predator Expert Testimony', *Psychiatric Times* (30 January 2015), n.p.

55 William M. Fleming, Brian Jory and David L. Burton, 'Characteristics of Juvenile Offenders Admitting to Sexual Activity with Nonhuman Animals', *Society and Animals*, X/1 (2002), pp. 31–45 (p. 42).

56 Mark Matthews, *The Horse-man: Obsessions of a Zoophile* (New York, 1994), p. 204.

57 Ibid., p. 20.

58 Ibid., p. 11.

59 James Serpell, *In the Company of Animals: A Study of Human–Animal Relationships* (Oxford, 1986), p. 174.

Four 'Zoo' Communities

1 Mark Matthews, *The Horse-man: Obsessions of a Zoophile* (New York, 1994), p. 206.

2 Rebecca Cassidy, 'Zoosex and Other Relationships with Animals', in *Transgressive Sex: Subversion and Control in Erotic Encounters*, ed. Hastings Donnan and Fiona Magowan (Oxford, 2009), pp. 92–112 (p. 108).

3 Ibid., pp. 92–112 (p. 97).

4 Matthews, *The Horse-man*, p. 159.

5 Ibid., p. 193.

6 Ibid., p. 200.

7 Ibid.

8 Ibid., p. 201.

9 Ibid., p. 206.

10 Ibid., pp. 206–7.

11 Ibid., p. 207.

12 Ibid.

13 Ibid., p. 201.

14 For example, see Hani Miletski, *Mother–Son Incest: The Unthinkable Broken Taboo. An Overview of Findings* (Brandon, VT, 1995).

15 Cited in Diane Richard, 'Forbidden Love', *Contemporary Sexuality: An International Resource for Educators, Researchers, and Therapists*, XXXV/10 (October 2001), pp. 1, 4–7 (p. 4).

16 Hani Miletski, 'Zoophilia: Implications for Therapy', *Journal of Sex Education and Therapy*, XXVI/2 (2001), pp. 85–9.

17 Damian Jacob Sendler, 'Why People Who Have Sex with Animals Believe That It Is Their Sexual Orientation: A Grounded Theory Study of Online Communities of Zoophiles', *Deviant Behavior*, XXXIX/11 (2018), pp. 1507–14 (p. 1508).

18 Damian Jacob Sendler and Michal Lew-Starowicz, 'Digital Ethnography of Zoophilia: A Multinational Mixed-method Study', *Journal of Sex and Marital Therapy*, XLV/4 (May 2018), pp. 1–77.

19 Sendler, 'Why People Who Have Sex with Animals Believe That It Is Their Sexual Orientation', pp. 1507–14 (p. 1509).

20 Hani Miletski, 'Introduction to Bestiality and Zoophilia', *Contemporary Sexuality*, XL/12 (2006), pp. 8–12 (p. 10).

21 Ibid.

22 Ibid.

23 Ibid.

24 Andrea Beetz, 'New Insights into Bestiality and Zoophilia', in *Bestiality and Zoophilia*, ed. Beetz and A. L. Podberscek (West Lafayette, IN, 2005), pp. 98–119.

25 Ibid.

26 Ibid.

27 Miletski, 'Introduction to Bestiality and Zoophilia', pp. 8–12 (p. 10).

28 Ibid.

29 Richard, 'Forbidden Love', pp. 1, 4–7 (p. 5).

30 Sendler and Lew-Starowicz, 'Digital Ethnography of Zoophilia', pp. 1–77 (p. 21).

31 Robert E. Jenkins and Alexander R. Thomas, *Deviance Online: Portrayals of Bestiality on the Internet* (New York, 2004), p. 45; R. J. Maratea, 'Screwing the Pooch: Legitimizing Accounts of a Zoophilic On-line Community', *Deviant Behavior*, XXXII/10 (2011), pp. 918–43 (p. 929); Sendler, 'Why People Who Have Sex with Animals Believe That It Is Their Sexual Orientation', pp. 1507–14 (p. 1510).

32 Colin J. Williams and Martin S. Weinberg, 'Zoophilia in Men: A Study of Sexual Interest in Animals', *Archives of Sexual Behavior*, XXXII/6 (2003), pp. 523–35 (p. 525).

33 Hani Miletski, *Understanding Bestiality and Zoophilia* (Bethesda, MD, 2002), p. 194.

34 Beetz, 'New Insights into Bestiality and Zoophilia', pp. 98–119.

35 Miletski, *Understanding Bestiality and Zoophilia*, p. 194.

36 Miletski, 'Zoophilia: Implications for Therapy', pp. 85–9 (p. 89).

37 Sendler, 'Why People Who Have Sex with Animals Believe That It Is Their Sexual Orientation', pp. 1507–14 (p. 1510).

38 Quoting 'Mark155', in Sendler, 'Why People Who Have Sex with Animals Believe That It Is Their Sexual Orientation', pp. 1507–14 (p. 1510).

39 Miletski, 'Introduction to Bestiality and Zoophilia', pp. 8–12 (p. 10).

40 Miletski, 'Zoophilia: Implications for Therapy', pp. 85–9 (p. 85).

41 Sendler and Lew-Starowicz, 'Digital Ethnography of Zoophilia', pp. 1–77 (p. 23); Sendler, 'Why People Who Have Sex with Animals Believe That It Is Their Sexual Orientation', pp. 1507–14 (p. 1510); Aronha e Silva de Souza, Renata Almeida and Danilo Antonio Baltieri, 'A Preliminary Model of Motivation for Pornography

Consumption among Men Participating in Zoophilic Virtual Environments', *Journal of Sex and Marital Therapy*, XLII/2 (2016), pp. 143–57 (p. 143).

42 Miletski, 'Introduction to Bestiality and Zoophilia', pp. 8–12 (p. 10).

43 Ibid.

44 Williams and Weinberg, 'Zoophilia in Men', pp. 523–35 (p. 526).

45 Beetz, 'New Insights into Bestiality and Zoophilia', pp. 98–119.

46 Cassidy, 'Zoosex and Other Relationships with Animals', pp. 91–112 (p. 101).

47 Sendler, 'Why People Who Have Sex with Animals Believe That It Is Their Sexual Orientation', pp. 1507–14 (pp. 1509 and 1511).

48 Zoophile Rights Day, Podiumsdiskussion 1 and 2. The discussion can be seen at www.youtube.com.

49 Olivier Burdinski talking to Dominic Mealy, in 'Forbidden Love', *Exberliner* (9 July 2014), at www.exberliner.com. This is also on YouTube at www.youtube. com, accessed 18 March 2019.

50 Ibid.

51 ZETA website, 'Representing the Interests of the Zoophile Community', at www.zeta-verein.de, accessed 2 February 2019.

52 Interview with Michael Kiok, 6 February 2019. This was in line with the estimate given by Burdinski talking to Mealy, in 'Forbidden Love', pp. 1, 4–7.

53 Sendler and Lew-Starowicz, 'Digital Ethnography of Zoophilia', pp. 1–77 (p. 23).

54 Sendler, 'Why People Who Have Sex with Animals Believe That It Is Their Sexual Orientation', pp. 1510–12, and Sendler and Lew-Starowicz, 'Digital Ethnography of Zoophilia', pp. 1–77 (p. 32).

55 Sendler, 'Why People Who Have Sex with Animals Believe That It Is Their Sexual Orientation', pp. 1510–14 (p. 1511).

56 Ibid.

57 Ibid.

58 Robert Edward Lee Masters, *Sex-driven People: An Autobiographical Approach to the Problem of the Sex-dominated Personality* (Los Angeles, CA, 1966), see pp. 127–8.

59 Miletski, 'Zoophilia: Implications for Therapy', pp. 85–9 (p. 87).

60 A film of him talking can be found in 'What Activists Are Doing to Fight the Rampant Growth of Bestiality', at https://melmagazine.com, accessed 20 January 2019.

61 Jia Tolentino, 'A Chat with Malcolm Brenner, Man Famous for Having Sex with a Dolphin', *Jezebel* (2 November 2015), at https://jezebel.com, accessed 5 May 2019.

62 Malcolm J. Brenner, *Wet Goddess: Recollections of a Dolphin Lover* [1974] (Punta Gorda, FL, 2009), n.p. Note that although he calls it 'a novel', it is based on his personal experiences, about which he has subsequently been interviewed.

63 Robert Edward Lee Masters, *Forbidden Sexual Behavior and Morality: An Objective Re-examination of Perverse Sex Practices in Different Cultures* (New York, 1962), pp. 46 and 82.

64 Hani Miletski, 'Is Zoophilia a Sexual Orientation?: A Study', *Journal of Sexual Medicine* (2005), pp. 82–97 (p. 89).

65 Sendler and Lew-Starowicz, 'Digital Ethnography of Zoophilia', pp. 1–77 (p. 23).

66 Miletski, 'Introduction to Bestiality and Zoophilia', pp. 8–12 (p. 10).

67 Maratea, 'Screwing the Pooch', pp. 918–43; Williams and Weinberg, 'Zoophilia in Men', pp. 523–35 (p. 526).

68 Miletski, 'Is Zoophilia a Sexual Orientation?', pp. 82–97 (p. 82).

69 Beetz, 'New Insights into Bestiality and Zoophilia', pp. 98–119.

70 Sendler and Lew-Starowicz, 'Digital Ethnography of Zoophilia', pp. 1–77 (p. 29).

71 Matthews, *The Horse-man*, p. 50.

72 Miletski, 'Introduction to Bestiality and Zoophilia', pp. 8–12 (p. 10).

73 P. O. Peretti and M. Rowan, 'Zoophilia: Factors Related to Its Sustained Practice', *Panminerva Medica: A Journal on Internal Medicine*, xxv/2 (1983), pp. 127–31.

74 'Hidden Love: Animal Passions', a documentary film, at www.youtube.com, accessed 5 May 2019.

75 Williams and Weinberg, 'Zoophilia in Men', pp. 523–35 (p. 526). Also see Maratea, 'Screwing the Pooch', pp. 918–43 (pp. 928–31).

76 Williams and Weinberg, 'Zoophilia in Men', pp. 523–35 (p. 529).

77 Ibid., pp. 523–35 (p. 526).

78 Ibid.

79 Sendler, 'Why People Who Have Sex with Animals Believe That It Is Their Sexual Orientation', pp. 1507–14 (p. 1511).

80 Ibid., pp. 1507–14 (p. 1512).

81 Sendler and Lew-Starowicz, 'Digital Ethnography of Zoophilia', pp. 1–77 (p. 26).

82 Christopher M. Earls and Martin L. Lalumière, 'A Case Study of Preferential Bestiality', *Archives of Sexual Behavior*, xxxviii/4 (2009), pp. 605–9 (p. 606).

83 N. Kenneth Sandnabb et al., 'Characteristics of a Sample of Sadomasochistically-orientated Males with Recent Experience of Sexual Contact with Animals', *Deviant Behavior: An Interdisciplinary Journal*, xxiii/6 (2002), pp. 511–29 (p. 525).

84 *Zoo* (2007, dir. Robinson Devor).

85 Peretti and Rowan, 'Zoophilia: Factors Relating to Its Sustained Practice', pp. 127–31 (p. 129).

86 A 'zoo' cited in Masters, *Sex-driven People*, pp. 124–5, 144 and 152.

87 Ibid., p. 125.

88 Ibid.

89 This pervades his memoir but, for example, see Matthews, *The Horse-man*, pp. 58, 91, 99–100, 110 and 170.

90 Ibid., p. 91. The tattoo can be seen in 'Hidden Love: Animal Passions', a documentary film, at www.youtube.com, accessed 5 May 2019.

91 Matthews, *The Horse-man*, p. 96.

92 This can be seen in the film *Zoo* (2007).

93 Masters, *Sex-driven People*, p. 156.

94 Cassidy, 'Zoosex and Other Relationships with Animals', pp. 91–112 (p. 107).

95 Richard, 'Forbidden Love', pp. 1, 4–7 (p. 7).

96 Cassidy, 'Zoosex and Other Relationships with Animals', pp. 91–112 (p. 105).

Five 'Z', or Post-human Love

1 J. R. Ackerley, *My Father and Myself* (London, 1968), p. 217.

2 J. R. Ackerley in the *New Statesman*, cited in Peter Parker, *Ackerley: A Life of J. R. Ackerley* (London, 1990), p. 261.

3 J. R. Ackerley, *My Dog Tulip* [1956] (New York, 1999), pp. 8–9.

4 Ibid., p. 44.

5 Ibid., p. 57.

6 Ibid., p. 20. In the book, she is named as Miss Canvey but her real name was Miss Woodyear.
7 Eve Kosofsky Sedgwick, *Epistemology of the Closet* (Los Angeles, CA, 1990), p. 168.
8 Ackerley, *My Dog Tulip*, p. 63.
9 Ibid., p. 71.
10 Ibid., p. 101.
11 Jonathan Balcombe, *Pleasurable Kingdom: Animals and the Nature of Feeling Good* (London, 2006), pp. 126–32; Jennifer Terry, '"Unnatural Acts" in Nature: The Scientific Fascination with Queer Animals', *GLQ: A Journal of Lesbian and Gay Studies*, VI/2 (2000), pp. 151–93 (p. 156); Robert Edward Lee Masters, *Forbidden Sexual Behavior and Morality: An Objective Re-examination of Perverse Sex Practices in Different Cultures* (New York, 1962), p. 77; Tony Milligan, 'The Wrongness of Sex with Animals', *Public Affairs Quarterly*, XXV/3 (July 2011), pp. 241–55 (p. 246).
12 Marc Bekoff and John A. Byers, eds, *Animal Play: Evolutionary, Comparative, and Ecological Perspectives* (Cambridge, 1999).
13 Balcombe, *Pleasurable Kingdom*, pp. 111–13; Antonio Haynes, 'The Bestiality Proscription: In Search of a Rationale', *Animal Law*, 21 (2014), pp. 121–50 (p. 129); Terry, '"Unnatural Acts" in Nature', pp. 151–93.
14 Balcombe, *Pleasurable Kingdom*, p. 111. Also see Jonathan Balcombe, *Second Nature: The Inner Lives of Animals* (London, 2010); Bekoff and Byers, eds, *Animal Play: Evolutionary, Comparative, and Ecological Perspectives*.
15 Bruce Bagemihl, *Biological Exuberance: Animal Homosexuality and Natural Diversity* (London, 1999).
16 Adam Smith, *The Theory of Moral Sentiments*, ed. Knud Haakonssen (Cambridge, 2002), pp. 11–12.
17 Thomas Nagel, 'What Is It Like to Be a Bat?', *Philosophical Review*, LXXXIII/4 (October 1974), pp. 435–50 (pp. 438, 440 and 442).
18 Ralph R. Acampora, 'Bodily Being and Animal World: Towards a Somatology of Cross-species Community', in *Animal Others: On Ethics, Ontology, and Animal Life*, ed. H. Peter Steeves (Albany, NY, 1999), pp. 117–31 (p. 118).
19 Gregory S. Berns, Andrew M. Brooks and Mark Spivak, 'Functional MRI in Awake Unrestrained Dogs', *PlosOne*, VII/5 (May 2012), pp. 1–6 (p. 1).
20 J. M. Coetzee, *The Lives of Animals*, ed. and intro. by Amy Gutmann (Princeton, NJ, 2001), p. 33.
21 Ibid., p. 35.
22 Ackerley, *My Dog Tulip*, pp. 56–7.
23 For a detailed discussion, see my *What It Means to Be Human: Historical Reflections from 1791 to the Present* (London, 2011).
24 Dana Shai and Jay Belsky, 'When Words Just Won't Do: Introducing Parental Embodiment Mentalizing', *Child Development Perspectives*, V/3 (2011), pp. 173–80 (p. 175). Also see Dana Shai and Jay Belsky, 'Parental Embodiment Mentalizing: Let's Be Explicit about What We Mean by Implicit', *Child Development Perspectives*, V/3 (2011), pp. 187–8.
25 For example, Anthony P. Atkinson, Mary L. Tunstall and Winand H. Dittrich, 'Evidence for Distinct Contributions of Form and Motion Information to the Recognition of Emotions from Body Gestures', *Cognition*, CIV/1 (2007), pp. 59–72; Elizabeth Crane and Melissa Gross, 'Motion Capture and Emotion:

Affect Detection in Whole Body Movement', *Affective Computing and Intelligent Interaction*, 28 (2007), pp. 95–101; R. Thomas Boone and Joseph G. Cunningham, 'Children's Decoding of Emotion in Expressive Body Movement: The Development of Cue Attunement', *Developmental Psychology*, XXXXIV/5 (1998), pp. 1007–16; Matthew J. Hertenstein, Rachel Holmes, Margaret McCullough and Dacher Keltner, 'The Communication of Emotion Via Touch', *Emotion*, IX/4 (2009), pp. 566–73.

26 Shai and Belsky, 'When Words Just Won't Do', pp. 173–80 (p. 176). Also see *The Meaning of Movement: Developmental and Clinical Perspectives of the Kestenberg Movement Profile*, ed. Janet Kestenberg Amighi, Susan Loman, Penny Lewis and K. Mark Sossin (Amsterdam, 1999); and Suzi Tortora, *The Dancing Dialogue: Using the Communicative Power of Movement with Young Children* (Baltimore, MD, 2006).

27 Shai and Belsky, 'When Words Just Won't Do', pp. 176–80 (p. 176).

28 Ibid., pp. 176–80 (p. 173).

29 For example, see Daniel Bernhardt and Peter Robinson, 'Detecting Affect from Non-stylised Body Motions', *Affective Computing and Intelligent Interaction* (September 2007), pp. 59–60; Ginevra Castellano, Santiago D. Villalba and Antonio Camurri, 'Recognising Human Emotions from Body Movement and Gesture Dynamics', ibid., pp. 71–82; Crane and Gross, 'Motion Capture and Emotion', ibid., pp. 95–101; Andrea Kleinsmith and Nadia Bianchi-Berthouze, 'Recognizing Affective Dimensions from Body Posture', ibid., pp. 48–58; Harald [*sic*] G. Wallbott, 'Bodily Expression of Emotion', *European Journal of Social Psychology*, XXVIII/6 (November–December 1998), pp. 879–96.

30 Atkinson, Tunstall and Dittrich, 'Evidence for Distinct Contributions of Form and Motion Information', pp. 59–72.

31 Gaddi Blumrosen, David Hawellek and Bijan Pesaran, 'Towards Automated Recognition of Facial Expression in Animal Models', *2017 IEEE International Conference on Computer Vision Workshops* (2018), pp. 2810–19.

32 For example, see S. Yin and B. McCowan, 'Barking in Domestic Dogs', *Animal Behaviour*, 68 (2004), pp. 343–55; Csaba Molnár et al., 'Classification of Dog Barks: A Machine Leaning Approach', *Animal Cognition*, XI/3 (2008), pp. 389–400; Péter Pongrácz et al., 'Human Listeners Are Able to Classify Dog (*Canis familiaris*) Barks Recorded in Different Situations', *Journal of Comparative Psychology*, CIX/2 (2005), pp. 136–44.

33 Yin and McCowan, 'Barking in Domestic Dogs', pp. 343–55.

34 Warongkhana Phanwanich et al., 'Animal-assisted Therapy for Persons with Disabilities Based on Canine Tail Language Interpretation Via Fuzzy Emotional Behavior Model', *33rd Annual International Conference of the IEEE EMS* (2011), pp. 1133–6 and Warongkhana Phanwanich et al., 'Animal-assisted Therapy for Persons with Disabilities Based on Canine Tail Language Interpretation via Gaussian-Trapezoidal Fuzzy Emotional Behavior Model', *World Academy of Science, Engineering, and Technology. International Journal of Animal and Veterinary Sciences*, V/11 (2011), pp. 578–82.

35 Simone Hantke, Nicholas Cumming and Björn Schuller, 'What Is My Dog Trying to Tell Me? The Automatic Recognition of the Context and Perceived Emotion of Dog Barks', *International Conference on Computing and Informatics* (2018), pp. 5134–8 (p. 5134).

36 Ibid.
37 Csaba Molnár et al., 'Can Humans Discriminate between Dogs on the Base of the Acoustic Parameters of Barks?', *Behavioral Processes*, LXXIII/1 (2006), pp. 76–83, and Péter Pongrácz, Adám Miklósi and Vilmos Csányi, 'Owners' Beliefs on the Ability of Their Pet Dogs to Understand Human Verbal Communication: A Case of Social Understanding', *Current Psychology of Cognition*, XX/1–2 (2001), pp. 87–108.
38 See Márta Gáci et al., 'Are Readers of our Faces Readers of Our Minds? Dogs (*Canis familiaris*) Show Situation-dependent Recognition', *Animal Cognition*, 7 (2004), pp. 144–53.
39 Antonio Lanata et al., 'A Case for the Interspecies Transfer of Emotions: A Preliminary Investigation on How Humans' Odors Modify Reactions of the Autonomic Nervous System in Horses', *Conference Proceedings: Annual International Conference of the IEEE Engineering in Medicine and Biology Society* (2018), p. 522.
40 I. Adachi, H. Kuwahata and K. Fujita, 'Dogs Recall Their Owner's Face', *Animal Cognition*, X/1 (2007), pp. 17–21. Also see Biagio D'Aniello et al., 'Interspecies Transmission of Emotion Information via Chemosignals: From Humans to Dogs (*Canis Lupus Familiaris*)', *Animal Cognition*, XXI/1 (2018), pp. 67–78; and Gün R. Semin, 'Grounding Communication: Synchrony', in *Social Psychology: Handbook of Basic Principles*, ed. Arie W. Kruglanski and E. Tory Higgins (New York, 2007), pp. 630–49.
41 Gregory Berns, *How Dogs Love Us: A Neuroscientist and His Dog Decode the Canine Brain* (London, 2014), pp. 173–4.
42 Ibid., p. 192.
43 Traci Warkentin, 'Interspecies Etiquette: An Ethics of Paying Attention to Animals', *Ethics and the Environment*, XV/1 (Spring 2010), pp. 101–21 (pp. 101–3).
44 Thomas J. Csordas, 'Somatic Modes of Attention', *Cultural Anthropology*, VIII/2 (May 1997), pp. 135–56 (p. 138).
45 Thomas J. Csordas, 'Embodiment and Cultural Phenomenology', in *Perspectives on Embodiment*, ed. Gail Weiss and Honi Haber (New York, 1999), pp. 143–62 (p. 148).
46 Kenneth J. Shapiro, 'A Phenomenological Approach to the Study of Nonhuman Animals', in *Anthropomorphism, Anecdotes, and Animals*, ed. Robert W. Mitchell, Nicholas S. Thompson and H. Lyn Miles (Albany, NY, 1997), pp. 277–95.
47 Ibid., p. 292.
48 Temple Grandin, *Thinking in Pictures and Other Reports from My Life with Autism* (London, 2006), p. 168. Also see Temple Grandin and Catherine Johnson, *Animals in Translation: Using the Mysteries of Autism to Decode Animal Behaviour* (London, 2005), p. 23.
49 Monty Roberts, *The Man Who Listens to Horses* (London, 1997). Also see Argent Gala, 'Toward a Privileging of the Nonverbal: Communication, Corporeal Synchrony, and Transcendence in Humans and Horses', in *Experiencing Animal Minds: An Anthology of Animal–Human Encounters*, ed. Julie A. Smith and Robert W. Mitchell (New York, 2012), pp. 111–28.
50 Florence Gaunet, 'How Do Guide Dogs and Pet Dogs (*Canis familiaris*) Ask Their Owners for Their Toys and for Playing?', *Animal Cognition*, XIII/2 (March 2010), pp. 311–23.
51 Barbara Smuts, 'Reflections', in Coetzee, *The Lives of Animals*, pp. 115–19.

52 Elizabeth A. Behnke, 'Ghost Gestures: Phenomenological Investigations of Bodily Micromovements and Their Intercorporeal Implications', *Human Studies*, 20 (1997), pp. 181–201.

53 Berns, *How Dogs Love Us*, p. 196.

54 Dana Shai and Peter Fonagy, 'Beyond Words: Parental Embodied Mentalizing and the Parent–Infant Dance' (2012), 13, at portal.idc.ac.il/en/symposium/hspsp/2012/documents/cshai12.pdf, viewed 8 February 2019.

55 Ackerley, *My Dog Tulip*, pp. 71–2.

56 Ackerley, *My Father and Myself*, pp. 217–18.

57 Donna Haraway, *The Companion Species Manifesto: Dogs, People, and Significant Otherness* (Chicago, IL, 2003), p. 2.

58 Kathy Rudy, 'LGBTQ-Z?', *Hypatia: A Journal of Feminist Philosophy*, XXVII/3 (Summer 2012), pp. 601–15 (p. 605).

59 Kathy Rudy, *Loving Animals: Towards a New Animal Advocacy* (Minneapolis, MN, 2011), p. xii.

60 Rudy, 'LGBTQ-Z?', pp. 601–15 (p. 605).

61 Ibid., pp. 601–15 (p. 611).

62 Haraway, *Companion Species Manifesto*, p. 12.

63 For instance, see R. G. Frey, 'Vivisection, Morals and Medicine', *Journal of Medical Ethics*, IX/2 (1983), pp. 94–7.

64 Eva Feder Kittay, 'Equality, Dignity, and Disability', in *Perspectives on Equality: The Second Seamus Heaney Lectures*, ed. Mary Ann Lyons and Fionnuala Waldron (Dublin, 2005), pp. 95–122.

65 Leslie Pickering Francis and Anita Silvers, 'Liberalism and Individually Scripted Ideas of the Good: Meeting the Challenge of Dependent Agency', *Social Theory and Practice*, XXXIII/2 (April 2007), pp. 311–34 (p. 311).

66 Ibid., pp. 311–34 (p. 322).

67 Fred Kaeser, 'Can People with Severe Mental Retardation Consent to Mutual Sex?', *Sexuality and Disability*, X/1 (1992), pp. 35–7.

68 Deborah W. Denno, 'Sexuality, Rape, and Mental Retardation', *University of Illinois Law Review*, CCCXV (1997), pp. 315–434 (p. 315).

69 Ibid., pp. 315–434 (p. 315).

70 Ibid., pp. 315–434 (p. 316).

71 For example, see John M. Niederbuhl and C. Donald Morris, 'Sexual Knowledge and the Capacity of Persons with Dual Diagnoses to Consent to Sexual Contact', *Sexuality and Disability*, XI (1993), pp. 295–307 (p. 305).

72 Francis and Silvers, 'Liberalism and Individually Scripted Ideas of the Good', *Social Theory and Practice*, XXXIII/2 (April 2007), pp. 311–34 (p. 331).

73 This was the decision of the New York Court of Appeals in *People v. Easley*, 364 N.E. 2d 1323, 1330–31 (New York, 1977) and *People v. Cratsley*, 653 N.W. 2d 1162–64 (New York, 1993).

74 Haynes, 'The Bestiality Proscription', pp. 121–50 (p. 149).

75 Ibid., pp. 121–50 (p. 149).

76 Joseph J. Fischel, 'Horse F#$@ing [*sic*] and the Limits of Consent: What *Broad City* Teaches Us about Sexual Violence', *Studies in Gender and Sexuality*, XVIII/1 (2017), pp. 31–4 (p. 32).

77 Margret Grebowicz, 'When Species Meat [*sic*]: Confronting Bestiality Pornography', *Humanimalia*, I/2 (Spring 2010), at www.depauw.edu.

78 Monika Bakke, 'The Predicament of Zoopleasures: Human-nonhuman Libidinal Relations', in *Animal Encounters*, ed. Tom Tyler and Manuela Rossini (Leiden, 2009), pp. 221–42 (p. 228).
79 Ibid., pp. 221–42 (p. 223).
80 Parker, *Ackerley*, pp. 379–80.
81 Sue Donaldson and Will Kymlicka, *Zoopolis: A Political Theory of Animal Rights* (Oxford, 2011), p. 109.

Select Bibliography

'8-step Guide to Artificially Inseminating a Dairy Cow', *Farmers' Weekly*
  (5 November 2015), at www.fwi.co.uk
Abel, Gene G., et al., 'Multiple Paraphilic Diagnoses among Sex Offenders',
  Bulletin of the American Academy of Psychiatry and Law, VI/2 (1988),
  pp. 153–68
—, and Joanne L. Rouleau, 'The Nature and Extent of Sexual Assault', in *Handbook
  of Sexual Assault*, ed. W. L. Marshall, D. R. Laws and H. G. Barbaree (New York,
  1990), pp. 9–21
Acampora, Ralph R., 'Bodily Being and Animal World: Towards a Somatology of
  Cross-species Community', in *Animal Others: On Ethics, Ontology, and Animal Life*,
  ed. H. Peter Steeves (Albany, NY, 1999), pp. 117–31
Ackerley, J. R., *My Dog Tulip* [1956] (New York, 1999)
—, *My Father and Myself* (London, 1968)
Adachi, I., H. Kuwahata and K. Fujita, 'Dogs Recall Their Owner's Face', *Animal
  Cognition*, X/1 (2007), pp. 17–21
Adams, Carol J., 'Woman-battering and Harm to Animals', in *Animals and Women:
  Feminist Theoretical Explorations*, ed. Adams and Josephine Donovan (Durham,
  1995), pp. 55–84
Aelian, *On the Characteristics of Animals*, trans. A. F. Schofield, I.1 and XVI.3
  (Cambridge, MA, 1958)
Aggrawal, Anil, 'A New Classification of Zoophilia', *Journal of Forensic and Legal
  Medicine*, 18 (2011), pp. 73–8
Almeida, Kelson James, et al., 'Zoophilia and Parkinson's Disease', *Parkinsonism and
  Related Disorders*, 19 (2013), pp. 1167–8
Alvarez, William A., and Jack P. Freinhar, 'A Prevalence Study of Bestiality (Zoophilia)
  in Psychiatric In-patients, Medical In-patients, and Psychiatric Staff', *International
  Journal of Psychosomatics*, 38 (1991), pp. 45–7
American Pet Products Association, 'Pet Industry Market Size and Ownership
  Statistics' (2018), at www.americanpetproducts.org
American Psychiatric Association, *Diagnostic and Statistical Manual of Mental Disorders*
  (Washington, DC, 1952)
—, *Diagnostic and Statistical Manual of Mental Disorders*, 3rd edn (Washington, DC, 1980)

—, *Diagnostic and Statistical Manual of Mental Disorders*, 3rd revd edn (Washington, DC, 1987)

—, *Diagnostic and Statistical Manual of Mental Disorders*, 4th edn (Washington, DC, 1994)

Amighi, Janet Kestenberg, et al., *The Meaning of Movement: Developmental and Clinical Perspectives of the Kestenberg Movement Profile* (Amsterdam, 1999)

Anderson, Rick, 'Closing the Barn Door', *Seattle Weekly* (9 November 2005), at www.seattleweekly.com

—, 'Here, Horsey! In 2005, the Seattle Times' Report on the Man Who Died', *Seattle Times* (20 April 2010), at www.seattleweekly.com

'Animal Crackers', *Wall Street Journal* (30 March 2001)

'Arizona Revised Statute 13, Criminal Code, 13-1411-C. Bestiality; Classification; Definition', at https://codes.findlaw.com, accessed 2 February 2019

Ascione, F. R., 'The Abuse of Animals and Human Interpersonal Violence', in *Child Abuse, Domestic Violence, and Animal Abuse*, ed. Ascione and P. Arkow (West Lafayette, IN, 1999), pp. 50–61

—, 'Children Who Are Cruel to Animals: A Review of Research and Implications for Developmental Psychopathology', in *Cruelty to Animals and Interpersonal Violence*, ed. L. Lockwood and Ascione (West Lafayette, IN, 1998), pp. 83–104

Atkinson, Anthony P., Mary L. Tunstall and Winand H. Dittrich, 'Evidence for Distinct Contributions of Form and Motion Information to the Recognition of Emotions from Body Gestures', *Cognition*, CIV/1 (2007), pp. 59–72

Bagemihl, Bruce, *Biological Exuberance: Animal Homosexuality and Natural Diversity* (London, 1999)

Baillet, Adrien, *La Vie de Monsieur Descartes*, vol. II (Paris, 1691)

Baker, Mike, 'Bill Banning Bestiality Gets Senate Hearing', *Associated Press State and Local News Wire* (1 February 2006), n.p.

Bakke, Monika, 'The Predicament of Zoopleasures: Human–Nonhuman Libidinal Relations', in *Animal Encounters*, ed. Tom Tyler and Manuela Rossini (Leiden, 2009), pp. 221–42

Balcombe, Jonathan, *Pleasurable Kingdom: Animals and the Nature of Feeling Good* (London, 2006)

—, *Second Nature: The Inner Lives of Animals* (London, 2010)

'Bamber Gascoigne: A Versatile One-man Band, Getting Faster', *The Times* (6 May 1977), p. 14

Beetz, Andrea M., 'Bestiality/Zoophilia: A Scarcely Investigated Phenomenon between Crime, Paraphilia, and Love', *Journal of Forensic Psychology Practice*, IV/2 (2004), pp. 1–36

—, 'New Insights into Bestiality and Zoophilia', in *Bestiality and Zoophilia*, ed. Andrea M. Beetz and A. L. Podberscek (West Lafayette, IN, 2005), pp. 98–119

Behnke, Elizabeth A., 'Ghost Gestures: Phenomenological Investigations of Bodily Micromovements and Their Intercorporeal Implications', *Human Studies*, 20 (1997), pp. 181–201

Beirne, Piers, 'On the Sexual Assault of Animals: A Sociological View', in *The Human/Animal Boundary: Historical Perspectives*, ed. Angela N. H. Creager and William Chester Jordon (New York, 2002), pp. 193–227

—, 'Rethinking Bestiality: Towards a Concept of Interspecies Sexual Assault', *Theoretical Criminology*, I/3 (1997), pp. 313–31

—, 'Rethinking Bestiality: Towards a Concept of Interspecies Sexual Assault',
    in *Companion Animals and Us: Exploring the Relationships between People and Pets*,
    ed. Anthony L. Podberscek, Elizabeth S. Paul and James A. Serpell (Cambridge,
    2000), pp. 313–31

Bekoff, Marc, and John A. Byer, *Animal Play: Evolutionary, Comparative, and
    Ecological Perspectives* (Cambridge, 1999)

Ben-Atar, Doron S., and Richard D. Brown, *Taming Lust: Crimes against Nature in the
    Early Republic* (Philadelphia, PA, 2014)

Bernhardt, Daniel, and Peter Robinson, 'Detecting Affect from Non-stylised Body
    Motions', *Affective Computing and Intelligent Interaction* (September 2007),
    pp. 59–60

Berns, Gregory, *How Dogs Love Us: A Neuroscientist and His Dog Decode the Canine
    Brain* (London, 2014)

Berns, Gregory S., Andrew M. Brooks and Mark Spivak, 'Functional MRI in Awake
    Unrestrained Dogs', *PlosOne*, VII/5, e38027 (May 2012), pp. 1–6

'Bestiality: Yes, It's a Crime', *Seattle Post-Intelligencer* (10 August 2005), p. B6

Bhatia, Manjeet Singh, Shruti Srivastava and Sumeet Sharma, 'An Uncommon
    Case of Zoophilia: A Case Report', *Medicine, Science, and the Law*, XLV/2 (2005),
    pp. 174–5

Blevins, Roger O., 'A Case of Severe Anal Injury in an Adolescent Male Due to
    Bestial Sexual Experimentation', *Journal of Forensic and Legal Medicine*, XVI/7
    (2009), pp. 403–6

Blumrosen, Gaddi, David Hawellek and Bijan Pesaran, 'Towards Automated
    Recognition of Facial Expression in Animal Models', *2017 IEEE International
    Conference on Computer Vision Workshops* (2018), pp. 2810–19

Bolliger, Gieri, and Antoine F. Goetschel, 'Sexual Relations with Animals
    (Zoophilia): An Unrecognized Problem in Animal Welfare Legislation', in
    Bestiality and Zoophilia: Sexual Relations with Animals, ed. Andrea M. Beetz and
    Anthony L. Podberscek (West Lafayette, IN, 2005), pp. 23–45

Boone, R. Thomas, and Joseph G. Cunningham, 'Children's Decoding of Emotion
    in Expressive Body Movement: The Development of Cue Attunement',
    Developmental Psychology, XXXIV/5 (1998), pp. 1007–16

Bourke, Joanna, *What It Means to Be Human: Historical Reflections from 1791 to the
    Present* (London, 2011)

Brenner, Malcolm J., *Wet Goddess: Recollections of a Dolphin Lover* [1974] (Punta
    Gorda, FL, 2009)

Brodeur, Nicole, 'Bestiality Bill Teaches Lesson in Restraint', *Seattle Times*
    (2 February 2006), p. B3

Brokenshire, Doug, *Washington State Place Names from Alki to Yelm* (Caldwell, ID,
    1993)

Brown, Laura, *Homeless Dogs and Melancholy Apes: Humans and Other Animals in the
    Modern Literary Imagination* (Ithaca, NY, 2010)

Bruce, Lenny, 'Psychopathia Sexualis', at www.youtube.com, accessed 15 March 2019

Bucchieri, Rebecca L., 'Bridging the Gap: The Connection between Violence against
    Animals and Violence against Humans', *Journal of Animal and Natural Resource
    Law*, II (2005), pp. 115–35

Burton, Sir Richard Francis, 'Foreword', in Count Roscaud, *Human Gorillas: A Study
    of Rape with Violence* (Paris, 1901), pp. i–viii

Casanova, Manuel F., Glenn Mannheim and Markus Kruesi, 'Hippocampal Pathology in Two Mentally Ill Paraphilics', *Psychiatric Research Neuroimaging*, CXV/1–2 (2002), pp. 79–89

Cassidy, Rebecca, 'Zoosex and Other Relationships with Animals', in *Transgressive Sex: Subversion and Control in Erotic Encounters*, ed. Hastings Donnan and Fiona Magowan (Oxford, 2009), pp. 91–112

Castellano, Ginevra, Santiago D. Villalba and Antonio Camurri, 'Recognising Human Emotions from Body Movement and Gesture Dynamics', *Affective Computing and Intelligent Interaction* (2007), pp. 71–82

Cerrone, Gerald H., 'Zoophilia in a Rural Population: Two Case Studies', *Journal of Rural Community Psychology*, XII/1 (Summer 1991), pp. 29–39

Clark, Doug, 'Bestiality Bill Flimsy Fodder from Capitol', *Spokesman Review* (15 January 2006), at www.spokesman.com, accessed 20 June 2019

Clifford, Edward Allen, *The Sexual Perversions and Abnormalities*, 2nd edn [1940] (London, 1949)

Cochran, William G., Frederick Mosteller and John W. Tukey, *Statistical Problems of the Kinsey Report on Sexual Behavior in the Human Male* (Washington, DC, 1954)

Coetzee, J. M., *The Lives of Animals*, ed. and intro. by Amy Gutmann (Princeton, NJ, 2001)

Cooper-Lehki, C., A. Schenk, C. M. Keelan and W. J. Fremouw, 'Underreporting of Bestiality among Juvenile Sex Offenders: Polygraph versus Self-report', *Journal of Forensic Sciences*, LIX/2 (2014), pp. 540–42

Cousins, Jane, *Make It Happy: What Sex Is All About* (London, 1978)

—, *Make It Happy: What Sex Is All About* (Harmondsworth, 1986)

Cousins-Mills, Jane, *Make It Happy, Make It Safe: What Sex Is All About* (London, 1988

—, '"Putting Ideas into Their Heads": Advising the Young', *Feminist Review*, 28 (January 1988), pp. 163–74)

Craig, I. D., 'Bestiality', *Police Surgeon: Journal of the Association of Police Surgeons of Great Britain*, 20 (November 1981), pp. 41–4

Crane, Elizabeth, and Melissa Gross, 'Motion-capture and Emotion', *Affective Computing and Intelligent Interaction*, 28 (2007), pp. 95–101

Csordas, Thomas J., 'Embodiment and Cultural Phenomenology', in *Perspectives on Embodiment*, ed. Gail Weiss and Honi Haber (New York, 1999), pp. 143–62

—, 'Somatic Modes of Attention', *Cultural Anthropology*, VIII/2 (May 1997), pp. 135–56

Cudworth, Erika, '"Most Farmers Prefer Blondes": Social Intersectionality and Species Relations', in *Humans and Other Animals*, ed. B. Carter and N. Charles (London, 2011), pp. 153–72

D'Aniello, Biagio, et al., 'Interspecies Transmission of Emotion Information via Chemosignals: From Humans to Dogs (*Canis lupus familiaris*)', *Animal Cognition*, XXI/1 (2018), pp. 67–78

Davis, Karen, 'Bestiality: Animal Liberation or Human License?', on United Poultry Concerns website (22 April 2001), at www.upc-online.org, accessed 10 January 2019

—, *The Holocaust and the Henmaid's Tale: A Case for Comparing Atrocities* (New York, 2005)

de Giorgio, Fabio, et al., 'Fatal Blunt Injuries Possibly Resulting from Sexual Abuse of a Calf: A Case Study', *Medicine, Science, and Law*, XLIX/4 (2009), pp. 307–10

de Souza, Aronha e Silva, Renata Almeida and Danilo Antonio Baltieri, 'A Preliminary Model of Motivation for Pornography Consumption among Men Participating in Zoophilic Virtual Environments', *Journal of Sex and Marital Therapy*, XLII/2 (2016), pp. 143–57

DeGioia, Phyllis, 'Recognizing Sexual Abuse in Animals', Vin News Service (5 March 2015), at news.vin.com, accessed 30 November 2018

Dekkers, Midas, *Dearest Pet: On Bestiality*, trans. Paul Vincent (London, 1994)

Denno, Deborah W., 'Sexuality, Rape, and Mental Retardation', *University of Illinois Law Review*, CCCXV (1997), pp. 315–434

Derrida, Jacques, 'The Animal That Therefore I Am (More to Follow)', *Critical Inquiry*, XXVIII/2 (Winter 2002), pp. 369–418

—, 'Force of Law: The "Mystical Foundations of Authority"', trans. Mary Quaintance, *Cardozo Law Review*, 11 (1990), pp. 919–1046

Derry, Margaret, *Masterminding Nature: The Breeding of Animals, 1750–2010* (Toronto, 2015)

Descartes, René, *Discourse on Method and Other Writings*, ed. F. E. Sutcliffe (Harmondsworth, 1968)

Donaldson, Sue, and Will Kymlicka, *Zoopolis: A Political Theory of Animal Rights* (Oxford, 2011)

Dubois-Desaulle, Gaston, *Bestiality: An Historical, Medical, Legal, and Literary Study*, trans. with addenda by 'A. F. N.' (New York, 1933)

Duffield, Gary, Angela Hassiotis and Eileen Vizard, 'Zoophilia in Young Sexual Abusers', *Journal of Forensic Psychiatry*, IX/2 (September 1998), pp. 294–304

Earls, Christopher M., and Martin L. Lalumière, 'A Case Study of Preferential Bestiality', *Archives of Sexual Behavior*, XXXVIII/4 (2009), pp. 605–9

East, W. Norwood, 'Sexual Offenders: A British View', *Yale Law Journal*, LV/3 (April 1946), pp. 527–57

Edwardes, Allen, and R.E.L. Masters, *The Cradle of Erotica: A Study of Afro-Asian Sexual Expression and an Analysis of Erotic Freedom in Social Relationships* (New York, 1963)

'Estimated Pet Population in the United Kingdom (UK) from 2009 to 2018', at www.statista.com, accessed 20 January 2018

Evans, Edward Payson, *The Criminal Prosecution and Capital Punishment of Animals* (London, 1906)

'The Fire Chief and the Sheep', *Smoking Gun* (4 January 2007), at www.thesmokinggun.com

'Fire Chief Caught on the Lamb', *Smoking Gun* (7 March 2006), at www.thesmokinggun.com

Fischel, Joseph J., 'Horse F#$@ing and the Limits of Consent: What *Broad City* Teaches Us about Sexual Violence', *Studies in Gender and Sexuality*, XVIII/1 (2017), pp. 31–4

Flavell, Shawna, 'Four More Former Iowa Pig Factory Farm Workers Admit Guilty', PETA website (24 June 2009), at www.peta.org

—, 'Sexual Abuse of Animals: A Recurring Theme on Factory Farms', PETA website (13 September 2010), at www.peta.org

Fleming, William M., Brian Jory and David L. Burton, 'Characteristics of Juvenile Offenders Admitting to Sexual Activity with Nonhuman Animals', *Society and Animals*, X/1 (2002), pp. 31–45

'Forbidden Love', *Exberliner* (9 July 2014), at www.exberliner.com

Fowler, Orson Squire, *Creative and Sexual Science; or, Manhood, Womanhood, and Their Mutual Relations* (London, 1904)

Frances, Allen, 'DSM5 and Sexual Disorders; Just Say No', *Psychiatric Times* (18 March 2010), n.p.

—, 'The Latest in Sexually Violent Predator Expert Testimony', *Psychiatric Times* (30 January 2015), n.p.

Francis, Leslie Pickering, and Anita Silvers, 'Liberalism and Individually Scripted Ideas of the Good: Meeting the Challenge of Dependent Agency', *Social Theory and Practice*, XXXIII/2 (April 2007), pp. 311–34

Freud, Sigmund, *Three Essays on the Theory of Sexuality*, trans. James Strachey (London, 1949)

Frey, R. G., 'Vivisection, Morals and Medicine', *Journal of Medical Ethics*, IX/2 (1983), pp. 94–7

Fudge, Erica, 'Monstrous Acts: Bestiality in Early Modern England', *History Today*, L/8 (August 2000), pp. 20–25

Gácsi, Márta, et al., 'Are Readers of Our Faces Readers of Our Minds? Dogs (*Canis familiaris*) Show Situation-dependent Recognition', *Animal Cognition*, VII/3 (2004), pp. 144–53

Gala, Argent, 'Toward a Privileging of the Nonverbal: Communication, Corporeal Synchrony, and Transcendence in Humans and Horses', in *Experiencing Animal Minds: An Anthology of Animal–Human Encounters*, ed. Julie A. Smith and Robert W. Mitchell (New York, 2012), pp. 111–28

Gaunet, Florence, 'How Do Guide Dogs and Pet Dogs (*Canis familiaris*) Ask Their Owners for Their Toys and for Playing?', *Animal Cognition*, XIII/2 (March 2010), pp. 311–23

Gott, Ted, and Kathryn Weir, *Gorilla* (London, 2012)

'Governor Signs Bill to Ban Bestiality', *Tucson Citizen* (24 May 2006)

Grandin, Temple, *Thinking in Pictures and Other Reports from My Life with Autism* (London, 2006)

—, and Catherine Johnson, *Animals in Translation: Using the Mysteries of Autism to Decode Animal Behaviour* (London, 2005)

Grebowicz, Margret, 'When Species Meat [sic]: Confronting Bestiality Pornography', *Humanimalia*, 1/2 (Spring 2010), at www.depauw.edu

Gregersen, Edgar, *Sexual Practices: The Story of Human Sexuality* (London, 1982)

Hall, Lee, 'Interwoven Threads: Some Thoughts on Professor Mackinnon's *Of Mice and Men*', UCLA *Women's Law Journal*, XIV/1 (2005), pp. 163–212

Hantke, Simone, Nicholas Cumming and Björn Schuller, 'What Is My Dog Trying to Tell Me? The Automatic Recognition of the Context and Perceived Emotion of Dog Barks', *International Conference on Computing and Informatics* (2018), pp. 5134–8

Haraway, Donna, *The Companion Species Manifesto: Dogs, People, and Significant Otherness* (Chicago, IL, 2003)

Haynes, Antonio, 'The Bestiality Proscription: In Search of a Rationale', *Animal Law*, 21 (2014), pp. 121–50

Hensley, Christopher, and Suzanne E. Tallichet, 'Animal Cruelty Motivations: Assessing Demographic and Situational Factors on Animal Cruelty Motivations', *Journal of Interpersonal Violence*, XX/11 (2005), pp. 1429–43

—, — and Erik L. Dutkiewicz, 'Examining Demographic and Situational Factors on Animal Cruelty Motivations', *International Journal of Offender Therapy and Comparative Criminology*, LX/3 (2010), pp. 492–502

—, — and S. D. Singer, 'Exploring the Possible Link between Childhood and Adolescent Bestiality and Interpersonal Violence', *Journal of Interpersonal Violence*, XXI/7 (2006), pp. 910–23

—, — and —, 'The Predictive Value of Childhood Animal Cruelty Methods on Later
    Adult Violence: Examining Demographic and Situational Correlates', *International
    Journal of Offender Therapy and Comparative Criminology*, LVI/2 (2012), pp. 281–95
Hertenstein, Matthew J., et al., 'The Communication of Emotion via Touch', *Emotion*,
    IX/4 (2009), pp. 566–73
'Hidden Love: Animal Passions', documentary film, at www.youtube.com, accessed
    5 May 2019
Hobbs, Christopher J., Helga G. I. Hanks and Jane M. Wynne, 'Sexual Abuse:
    The Scope of the Problem', in *Child Abuse and Neglect: A Clinician's Handbook*,
    2nd edn, ed. Hobbs, Hanks and Wynne (London, 1999), pp. 165–89
Home Office, *Setting the Boundaries: Reforming the Law of Sexual Offences* (London, 2000)
Horn, Jack C., and Jeff Meer, 'The Pleasure of Their Company: PT Survey Report on
    Pets', *Psychology Today*, XVIII/8 (August 1984), pp. 52–9
House, Ian, 'Harrison on Animal Pain', *Philosophy*, LXVI/257 (July 1991), pp. 376–9
Hunt, Morton M., *Sexual Behavior in the 1970s* (Chicago, IL, 1974)
Hurn, Samantha, *Human and Other Animals: Cross-cultural Perspectives on Human–
    Animal Interactions* (London, 2012)
Hvozdík, Anton, et al., 'Ethological, Psychological, and Legal Aspects of Animal
    Sexual Abuse', *Veterinary Journal*, CLXXII/2 (2006), pp. 374–6
Imbschweiler, I., et al., 'Animal Sexual Abuse in a Female Sheep', *Veterinary Journal*,
    CLXXXII/3 (2009), pp. 481–3
Jenkins, Robert E., and Alexander R. Thomas, *Deviance Online: Portrayals of Bestiality
    on the Internet* (New York, 2004)
Johnson, Luke, 'Rick Santorum Defends Interview Linking Homosexuality to "Man
    on Dog" Sex', *Huffington Post* (1 May 2012)
Kaeser, Fred, 'Can People with Severe Mental Retardation Consent to Mutual Sex?',
    Sexuality and Disability, X/1 (1992), pp. 35–7
Kant, Immanuel, *Groundwork of the Metaphysics of Morals*, trans. and ed. Mary Gregor
    and Jens Timmerman (Cambridge, 2012)
—, *Lectures on Ethics*, trans. P. Heath (Cambridge, 1997)
Kinsey, Alfred C., et al., *Sexual Behavior in the Human Female* (Bloomington, IN, 1953)
—, Wardell B. Pomeroy and Clyde E. Martin, *Sexual Behavior in the Human Male*
    (Philadelphia, PA, 1948)
Kirnov, Gueno K., Julian E. Losanoff and Kirren T. Kjossev, 'Zoophilia: A Rare Case of
    Traumatic Injury to the Rectum', *Injury: International Journal of Care of the Injured*,
    XXXIII/4 (2002), pp. 367–8
Kittay, Eva Feder, 'Equality, Dignity, and Disability', in *Perspectives on Equality:
    The Second Seamus Heaney Lectures*, ed. Mary Ann Lyons and Fionnuala Waldron
    (Dublin, 2005), pp. 95–122
Kleinsmith, Andrea, and Nadia Bianchi-Berthouze, 'Recognizing Affective Dimensions
    from Body Posture', *Affective Computing and Intelligent Interaction* (2007), pp. 48–58
Lanata, Antonio, et al., 'A Case for the Interspecies Transfer of Emotions:
    A Preliminary Investigation on How Humans' Odors Modify Reactions of
    the Autonomic Nervous System in Horses', Conference Proceedings. Annual
    International Conference of the IEEE Engineering in Medicine and Biology Society
    (2018), p. 522
Lesandrić, Vinka, et al., 'Zoophilia as an Early Sign of Psychosis', *Alcoholism and
    Psychiatry Research*, 53 (2017), pp. 27–32

Levack, Brian P., 'The Prosecution of Sexual Crimes in Early Eighteenth Century Scotland', *Scottish Historical Review*, LXXXIX/228 (October 2010), pp. 172–93

Levitt, Lacey, Tia A. Hoffer and Ann B. Loper, 'Criminal Histories of a Subsample of Animal Cruelty Offenders', *Aggression and Violent Behavior*, 30 (2016), pp. 45–58

Levy, David, *Love + Sex with Robots: The Evolution of Human–Robot Relationships* (London, 2008)

Liliequist, Jonas, 'Peasants against Nature: Crossing the Boundaries between Man and Animals in Seventeenth and Eighteenth Century Sweden', *Journal of the History of Sexuality*, I/3 (January 1991), pp. 393–423

Lilly, John C., *Communication between Man and Dolphin: The Possibilities of Talking with Other Species* (New York, 1978)

—, *Man and Dolphin* (London, 1962)

Long, Edward, *The History of Jamaica; or, General Survey of the Antient and Modern State of That Island with Reflections on Its Situation, Settlements, Inhabitants, Climate, Products, Commerce, Laws, and Government*, vol. II (London, 1774)

Lovelace, Linda, with Mike McGrady, *Ordeal* [1980] (London, 1981)

Lucian of Samosata, *True History: and Lucius; or, The Ass*, trans. Paul Turner (London, 1958)

McInerny, Ralph, 'Animal Husbandry', *Catholic Thing* (3 September 2008), at www.thecatholicthing.org

Mackinnon, Catharine A., 'Of Mice and Men: A Feminist Fragment on Animal Rights', in *Animal Rights: Current Debates and New Directions*, ed. Cass R. Sunstein and Martha Craven Nussbaum (Oxford, 2004), pp. 263–76

McNally, Richard J., and Brian M. Lukach, 'Behavioral Treatment of Zoophilic Exhibitionism', *Journal of Behavioral Therapy and Experimental Psychology*, XXII/4 (1991), pp. 281–4

Malamud, Randy, *An Introduction to Animals and Visual Culture* (Basingstoke, 2012)

Malhiot, Emily, 'Chapter 86: Nevada Finally Outlaws Bestiality', *University of the Pacific Law Review*, 49 (2017), pp. 556–73

Maratea, 'R. J., Screwing the Pooch: Legitimizing Accounts of a Zoophilic On-line Community', *Deviant Behavior*, XXXIII/10 (2011), pp. 918–43

'Marry Your Pet', at www.marryyourpet.com, accessed 5 March 2019

Masters, Robert Edward Lee, *Forbidden Sexual Behavior and Morality: An Objective Re-examination of Perverse Sex Practices in Different Cultures* (New York, 1962)

—, *Sex-driven People: An Autobiographical Approach to the Problem of the Sex-dominated Personality* (Los Angeles, CA, 1966)

Matthews, Mark, *The Horse-man: Obsessions of a Zoophile* (New York, 1994)

Maxwell-Stuart, P. G., '"Wild, Filthie, Execrabill, Detestabill, and Unnatural Sin": Bestiality in Early Modern Scotland', in *Sodomy in Early Modern Europe*, ed. Tom Betteridge (Manchester, 2002), pp. 82–93

Meer, Jeff, 'Pet Theories: Facts and Figures to Chew On', *Psychology Today*, XVIII/8 (August 1984), pp. 60–67

Menniger, K. A., 'Totemic Aspects of Contemporary Attitudes towards Animals', in *Psychoanalysis and Culture: Essays in Honor of Géza Róheim*, ed. G. B. Wilbur and W. Muensterberger (New York, 1951), pp. 42–74

Merck, Melinda, *Veterinary Forensics: Animal Cruelty Investigations* (Ames, IA, 2007)

Milam, Jennifer, 'Rococo Representations of Interspecies Sensuality and the Pursuit of Volupté', *Art Bulletin*, XCVII/2 (2015), pp. 192–209

Miletski, Hani, 'Introduction to Bestiality and Zoophilia', *Contemporary Sexuality*, XL/12 (2006), pp. 8–12

—, 'Is Zoophilia a Sexual Orientation: A Study', *Journal of Sexual Medicine* (2005), pp. 82–97

—, *Mother–son Incest: The Unthinkable Broken Taboo. An Overview of Findings* (Brandon, VT, 1995)

—, 'Zoophilia: Implications for Therapy', *Journal of Sex Education and Therapy*, XXVI/2 (2001), pp. 85–9

Miller, Karla S., and John F. Knutson, 'Reports of Severe Physical Punishment and Exposure to Animal Cruelty by Inmates Convicted of Felonies and by University Students', *Child Abuse and Neglect*, XXI/1 (1997), pp. 59–82

Milligan, Tony, 'The Wrongness of Sex with Animals', *Public Affairs Quarterly*, XXV/3 (July 2011), pp. 241–55

Mizelle, Brett, *Pig* (London, 2011)

Molnár, Csaba, et al., 'Can Humans Discriminate between Dogs on the Base of the Acoustic Parameters of Barks?', *Behavioral Processes*, LXXIII/1 (2006), pp. 76–83

—, et al., 'Classification of Dog Barks: A Machine Leaning Approach', *Animal Cognition*, XI/3 (2008), pp. 389–400

Money, John, *Lovemap: Clinical Concepts of Sexual/Erotic Health and Pathology, Paraphilia, and Gender Transposition in Childhood, Adolescence, and Maturity* (New York, 1986)

Morriss, Peter, 'Blurred Boundaries', *Inquiry: An Interdisciplinary Journal of Philosophy*, 40 (1997), pp. 259–89

Moskowitz, Peter, 'Idaho Gov. Signs "Ag Gag" Bill into Law', *Al Jazeera America* (2014), at http://america.aljazeera.com, accessed 15 March 2019

'MP Supports Parents over Sex Education', *The Times* (9 February 1980), p. 3

Mudede, Charles, 'Revisiting the Town of the Most Famous Horse Sex Death in Recorded History', *The Stranger* (22 July 2015), at www.thestranger.com

Munro, Helen M. C., 'Animal Sexual Abuse: A Veterinary Taboo?', *Veterinary Journal*, CLXXII/2 (2006), pp. 195–7

—, and M. V. Thrusfield, '"Battered Pets": Non-accidental Injuries Found in Dogs and Cats', *Journal of Small Animal Practice*, XLII/6 (June 2001), pp. 279–90

—, and —, 'Battered Pets: Sexual Abuse', in *Bestiality and Zoophilia: Sexual Relations with Animals*, ed. Andrea M. Beetz and Anthony L. Podberscek (West Lafayette, IN, 2005), pp. 71–81

Munro, Ranald, and Helen M. C. Munro, *Animal Abuse and Unlawful Killing: Forensic Veterinary Pathology* (Edinburgh, 2008)

Mussin, John M., '"Things Fearful to Name": Bestiality in Early America', in *The Animal/Human Boundary: Historical Perspectives*, ed. Angela N. H. Creager and William Chester Jordan (New York, 2002), pp. 115–56

Nagel, Thomas, 'What Is It Like to Be a Bat?', *Philosophical Review*, LXXXIII/4 (October 1974), pp. 435–50

Navarro, John C., and Richard Tweksbury, 'Bestiality: An Overview and Analytic Discussion', *Sociology Compass*, IX/10 (2015), pp. 864–75

Nelson, Rob, 'Interviews: The Dark Horse', *Cinema Scope*, at http://cinema-scope.com, accessed 15 March 2019

Niederbuhl, John M., and C. Donald Morris, 'Sexual Knowledge and the Capacity of Persons with Dual Diagnoses to Consent to Sexual Contact', *Sexuality and Disability*, XI (1993), pp. 295–307

'No Sex with Animals: Ohio Enacts Bestiality Law', *Spokesman Review* (27 March 2017), at www.spokesman.com

Nowicki, Stacy A., 'On the Lamb: Toward a National Animal Abusers Registry', *Animal Law*, 17 (2010), pp. 197–242

'Onwards and Upwards with the Arts', *New Criterion* (February 2007), p. 3

Paasonen, Susanna, 'The Beast Within: Materiality, Ethics, and Animal Porn', in *Controversial Images*, ed. F. Attwood et al. (London, 2013), pp. 201–14

Parker, Peter, *Ackerley: A Life of J. R. Ackerley* (London, 1990)

Pepys, Samuel, *The Diary of Samual Pepys* [1661] (Coln St Aldwyns, 2006)

Peretti, P. O., and M. Rowan, 'Zoophilia: Factors Related to Its Sustained Practice', *Panminerva Medica: A Journal on Internal Medicine*, XXV/2 (1983), pp. 127–31

Phanwanich, Warongkhana, et al., 'Animal-assisted Therapy for Persons with Disabilities Based on Canine Tail Language Interpretation via Fuzzy Emotional Behavior Model', *33rd Annual International Conference of the IEEE EMS* (2011), pp. 1133–6

—, et al., 'Animal-assisted Therapy for Persons with Disabilities Based on Canine Tail Language Interpretation via Gaussian-Trapezoidal Fuzzy Emotional Behavior Model', *World Academy of Science, Engineering, and Technology. International Journal of Animal and Veterinary Sciences*, V/11 (2011), pp. 578–82

'Police Deny Allegation by Shepherd', *The Times* (24 May 1985), p. 2

Pongrácz, Péter, et al., 'Human Listeners Are Able to Classify Dog (*Canis familiaris*) Barks Recorded in Different Situations', *Journal of Comparative Psychology*, CXIX/2 (2005), pp. 136–44

—, Adám Miklósi and Vilmos Csányi, 'Owners' Beliefs on the Ability of Their Pet Dogs to Understand Human Verbal Communication: A Case of Social Understanding', *Current Psychology of Cognition*, XX/1–2 (2001), pp. 87–108

Pope, Alexander, *The Rape of the Lock*, Canto 1, at www.gutenberg.org, accessed 10 June 2019

Prohibiting Obscene Animal Crush Videos in the Wake of United States v. Stevens. Hearing before the Committee on the Judiciary United States Senate One Hundred Eleventh Congress. Second Session. September 15, 2010. Serial No. J–111–108 (Washington, DC, 2011)

Rampling, Charlotte, *Charlotte Rampling: With Compliments* (London, 1987)

Ranger, Rebekah, and Paul Federoff, 'Commentary: Zoophilia and the Law', *Journal of the American Academy of Psychiatry and the Law*, XLII/4 (2014), pp. 421–6

Raven, David, 'Woman Who Had Sex with DOLPHIN during Lab Experiments Speaks Out for the First Time', *The Mirror* (9 June 2014), at www.mirror.co.uk

Regan, Tom, *The Case for Animal Rights* (London, 1983)

Richard, Diane, 'Forbidden Love', *Contemporary Sexuality: An International Resource for Educators, Researchers, and Therapists*, XXXV/10 (October 2001), pp. 1, 4–7

Riley, Christopher, 'The Dolphin Who Loved Me: The Nasa-funded Project That Went Wrong', *The Guardian* (8 June 2014), at www.theguardian.com, accessed 18 March 2019

Rimm, Marty, 'Marketing Pornography on the Information Superhighway: A Survey of 917,410 Images, Descriptions, Short Stories, and Animations Downloaded 8.5 Million Times by Consumers in over 2,000 Cities in Forty Countries, Provinces, and Territories', *Georgetown Law Journal*, 83 (1994–5), pp. 1849–934

Robert, Jason Scott, and Francoise Baylis, 'Crossing Species Boundaries', *American Journal of Bioethics*, III/3 (Summer 2003), pp. 1–13

Roberts, Michael, 'The Unjustified Prohibition against Bestiality: Why the Laws in Opposition Can Find No Support in the Harm Principle', *Journal of Animal and Environmental Law*, 1 (2009–10), pp. 176–221

Roberts, Monty, *The Man Who Listens to Horses* (London, 1997)

Roche, Philip Q., 'Sexual Deviations', *Federal Probation*, 14 (1950), pp. 3–11

Roesler, Richard, 'Senate Bill Would Ban Bestiality', *Spokesman Review* (13 January 2006), at www.spokesman.com, accessed 6 January 2019

Roscaud, Count, *Human Gorillas: A Study of Rape with Violence* (Paris, 1901)

Rosenberg, Gabriel, 'How Meat Changed Sex: The Law of Interspecies Intimacy after Industrial Production', GLQ, XXIII/4 (2017), pp. 473–506

Rudy, Kathy, 'LGBTQ-Z?', *Hypatia: A Journal of Feminist Philosophy*, XXVII/3 (Summer 2012), pp. 601–15

—, *Loving Animals: Towards a New Animal Advocacy* (Minneapolis, MN, 2011)

Ruskin, Samuel H., 'Analysis of Sex Offenses among Male Psychiatric Patients', *American Journal of Psychiatry*, XCVII/4 (January 1941), pp. 955–68

Salisbury, Joyce E., *The Beast Within: Animals in the Middle Ages* (New York, 1994)

Sandnabb, N. Kenneth, et al., 'Characteristics of a Sample of Sadomasochistically-orientated Males with Recent Experience of Sexual Contact with Animals', *Deviant Behavior: An Interdisciplinary Journal*, XXIII/6 (2002), pp. 511–29

Schaefer, Jim, 'Sheep Abuser Is Center of Debate: Man Fights Inclusion on Sex Offender Registry', *Detroit Free Press*, B1 (3 March 2006), at www.ar15.com

Sedgwick, Eve Kosofsky, *Epistemology of the Closet* (Los Angeles, CA, 1990)

Semin, Gün R., 'Grounding Communication: Synchrony', in *Social Psychology: Handbook of Basic Principles*, ed. Arie W. Kruglanski and E. Tory Higgins (New York, 2007), pp. 630–49

Sendler, Damien Jacob, 'Similar Mechanisms of Traumatic Rectal Injuries in Patients Who Had Anal Sex with Animals to Those Who Were Butt-fisted by Human Sexual Partner', *Journal of Forensic and Legal Medicine*, 51 (2017), pp. 69–73

—, 'Why People Who Have Sex with Animals Believe That It Is Their Sexual Orientation: A Grounded Theory Study of Online Communities of Zoophiles', *Deviant Behavior*, XXXIX/11 (2018), pp. 1507–14

—, and Michal Lew-Starowicz, 'Digital Communities of People with Paraphilia: A Study of Zoophiles', *25th European Congress of Psychiatry/European Psychiatry* (2017), 41S

—, and —, 'Digital Ethnography of Zoophilia: A Multinational Mixed-method Study', *Journal of Sex and Marital Therapy* (2018), pp. 1–77

—, and —, 'Motivation of Sexual Relationship with Animals: Study of a Multinational Group of 345 Zoophiles', *25th European Congress of Psychiatry/European Psychiatry*, 41S (2017), p. S852

—, and —, 'Rethinking Classification of Zoophilia', *25th European Congress of Psychiatry/European Psychiatry*, 41S (2017), p. S851

Serpell, James, *In the Company of Animals: A Study of Human–Animal Relationships* (Oxford, 1986)

Shai, Dana, and Jay Belsky, 'Parental Embodiment Mentalizing: Let's Be Explicit about What We Mean by Implicit', *Child Development Perspectives*, V/3 (2011), pp. 187–8

—, and —, 'When Words Just Won't Do: Introducing Parental Embodiment Mentalizing', *Child Development Perspectives*, V/3 (2011), pp. 173–80

—, and Peter Fonagy, 'Beyond Words: Parental Embodied Mentalizing and the Parent–Infant Dance' (2012), 13, at portal.idc.ac.il/en/symposium/hspsp/2012/documents/cshai12.pdf, viewed 8 February 2019

Shapiro, Kenneth J., 'A Phenomenological Approach to the Study of Nonhuman Animals', in *Anthropomorphism, Anecdotes, and Animals*, ed. Robert W. Mitchell, Nicholas S. Thompson and H. Lyn Miles (Albany, NY, 1997), pp. 277–95

Shea, Matthew, 'Punishing Animal Rights Activists for Animal Abuse: Rapid Reporting and the New Wave of AgGag [sic] Laws', *Columbia Journal of Law and Social Problems*, XLVIII/3 (2015), pp. 337–8

Shell, Marc, 'The Family Pet', *Representations*, 15 (Summer 1986), pp. 121–53

Shenken, L., 'Psychotherapy in a Case of Bestiality', *American Journal of Psychotherapy*, 14 (1960), pp. 728–40

Sikva, Cristina, 'Once Again, Legislature Fails to Outlaw Bestiality', *St Petersburg Times* (6 May 2010), p. 6

Sinclair, Leslie, Melinda Merck and Randall Lockwood, *Forensic Investigation of Animal Cruelty: A Guide for Veterinary and Law Enforcement Professionals* (Washington, DC, 2006)

Singer, Peter, 'Heavy Petting' (2001), at www.nerve.com

Singh, B. Sardar, *A Manual of Medical Jurisprudence for Police Officers* (Moradabad, 1916)

Smith, Adam, *The Theory of Moral Sentiments*, ed. Knud Haakonssen (Cambridge, 2002)

Smith, Wesley J., 'Horse Sense', *Weekly Standard* (30 August 2005), at www.weeklystandard.com

Smith-Howard, Kendra, *Pure and Modern Milk: An Environmental History since 1900* (New York, 2013)

Smuts, Barbara, 'Reflections', in J. M. Coetzee, *The Lives of Animals*, ed. and intro. by Amy Gutmann (Princeton, NJ, 2001), pp. 115–19

Stafford, Kevin J., and David J. Mellor, 'Painful Husbandry Procedures in Livestock and Poultry', in *Improving Animal Welfare: A Practical Approach*, ed. Temple Grandin (Wallingford, Oxfordshire, 2010), pp. 88–113

Stekel, Wilhelm, *Patterns of Psychosexual Infantilism*, ed. Emil A. Gutheil (New York, 1952)

Stevenson, Jack, 'Dead Famous: The Life and Movies of Erotic Cinema's Most Exploited Figure, Bodil Joensen', in *Fleshpot: Cinema's Sexual Myth Makers and Taboo Breakers*, ed. Stevenson (Manchester, 2000), p. 180

Story, Marilyn D., 'A Comparison of University Student Experience with Various Sexual Outlets in 1974 and 1980', *Adolescence*, XVII/68 (Winter 1982), pp. 727–47

Taylor, Timothy, *The Prehistory of Sex: Four Million Years of Human Sexual Culture* (London, 1996)

Terry, Jennifer, '"Unnatural Acts" in Nature: The Scientific Fascination with Queer Animals', *GLQ: A Journal of Lesbian and Gay Studies*, VI/2 (2000), pp. 151–93

Thoinot, Léon-Henri, *Medicolegal Aspects of Moral Offenses*, trans. Arthur Wisswold Weysse (Philadelphia, PA, 1911)

—, *Medicolegal Aspects of Moral Offenses*, trans. and enlarged Arthur Wisswold Weysse (Philadelphia, PA, 1913)

Thomas, Courtney, '"Not Having God before His Eyes": Bestiality in Early Modern England', *Seventeenth Century*, XXVI/1 (2011), pp. 149–73

Tolentino, Jia, 'A Chat with Malcolm Brenner, Man Famous for Having Sex with a Dolphin', *Jezebel* (2 November 2015), at https://jezebel.com

Tortora, Suzi, *The Dancing Dialogue: Using the Communicative Power of Movement with Young Children* (Baltimore, MD, 2006)

Traill, Thomas Stewart, 'Observations on the Anatomy of the Orang Outang', *Memoirs of the Wernerian Natural History Society*, 3 (1821), n.p.

Vincent, Norah, 'You're an Animal', *Village Voice* (26 March 2001), n.p.

Virgilio, Edoardo, Ester Franzese and Salvatore Caterino, 'Zoosexuality: An Unusual Case of Colorectal Injury', *Acta Chirurgica Belgica*, CXVI/5 (2016), pp. 316–18

Vizard, Eileen, 'Zoophilia in Young Sexual Abusers', *Journal of Forensic Psychiatry*, IX/2 (September 1998), pp. 294–304

von Krafft-Ebing, Richard, *Psychopathia Sexualis: A Medico-forensic Study* [1886] (London, 1939)

Wallbott, Harald [sic] G., 'Bodily Expression of Emotion', *European Journal of Social Psychology*, XXVIII/6 (November–December 1998), pp. 879–96

Warkentin, Traci, 'Interspecies Etiquette: An Ethics of Paying Attention to Animals', *Ethics and the Environment*, XV/1 (Spring 2010), pp. 101–21

'Washington Senate OKs Bestiality Bill', *Spokesman Review* (12 February 2006), at www.spokesman.com

Washington State Legislature, Section 1 SS8 RCW 16.52.205, at https://apps.leg.wa.gov, accessed 6 January 2019

West, W. Norwood, 'Sexual Offenders: A British View', *Yale Law Journal*, LV/3 (April 1946), pp. 527–57

'What Activists Are Doing to Fight the Rampant Growth of Bestiality', at https://melmagazine.com, accessed 20 January 2019

Wilcox, Daniel T., Caroline M. Foss and Marguerite L. Donathy, 'A Case Study of a Male Sex Offender with Zoosexual Interests and Behaviors', *Journal of Sexual Aggression*, XI/3 (September 2005), pp. 305–17

—, — and —, 'Working with Zoosexual Offenders (Addressing High Levels of Deviance)', in *Sex Offender Treatment: A Case Study Approach to Issues and Interventions*, ed. Wilcox, Tanya Garrett and Leigh Harkins (Chichester, 2015), pp. 242–66

Williams, Colin J., and Martin S. Weinberg, 'Zoophilia in Men: A Study of Sexual Interest in Animals', *Archives of Sexual Behavior*, XXXII/6 (2003), pp. 523–35

Wisch, Rebecca F., 'Table of State Animal Sexual Assault Law', *Animal Legal and Historical Center* (2016), at www.animallaw.info

Yin, S., and B. McCowan, 'Barking in Domestic Dogs', *Animal Behaviour*, 68 (2004), pp. 343–55

Zequi, Stênio de Cássio, 'The Medical Consequences of Sex between Humans and Animals', in *Sexual Diversity and Sexual Offending: Research, Assessments, and Clinical Treatment in Psychosexual Therapy*, ed. Glyn Hudson Allez (London, 2014), pp. 183–202

—, G. C. Guimarães and F. P. da Fonseca, 'Sex with Animals (SWA): Behavioral Characteristics and Possible Association with Penile Cancer. A Multicenter Study', *Journal of Sexual Medicine*, IX/7 (2012), pp. 1860

ZETA, 'Representing the Interests of the Zoophile Community', at www.zeta-verein.de, accessed 2 February 2019

Acknowledgements

Many thanks to all the people who read draft chapters, listened to me as I tried out ideas, and critiqued my arguments.

Photo Acknowledgements

Index